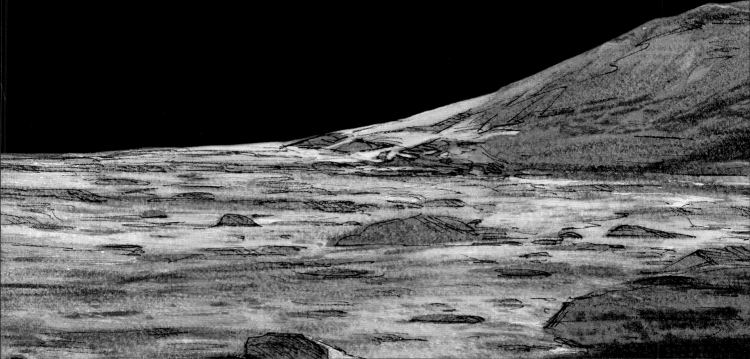

To everyone who has ever contributed
(even in a small way) to making the dream
of space exploration and travel a reality.
Thank you. *Ad Astra*

—Jennifer Swanson

Who Owns the Moon?

AND OTHER CONUNDRUMS OF EXPLORING AND USING SPACE

CYNTHIA LEVINSON

AND

JENNIFER SWANSON

MARGARET QUINLIN BOOKS

PEACHTREE
ATLANTA

Ω

Margaret Quinlin Books
An imprint of Peachtree Publishing Company Inc.
1700 Chattahoochee Avenue
Atlanta, Georgia 30318-2112
PeachtreeBooks.com

Text © 2025 by Cynthia Levinson and Jennifer Swanson
Jacket illustration © 2025 by Thomas Gonzalez
Illustrations © 2025 by Thomas Gonzalez
Spot illustrations and diagrams by Edward Miller
Maps and timelines by Trish Parcell

Design and composition by Trish Parcell
Jacket design by Thomas Gonzalez and Lily Steele
Edited by Margaret M. Quinlin

The illustrations by Thomas Gonzalez are watercolor base with watercolor
and regular color pencils, finished with fine tip marker ink lines.

Printed and bound in September 2024
at Papercraft Sdn Bhd in Malaysia
10 9 8 7 6 5 4 3 2 1
First Edition
ISBN: 978-1-68263-537-7
Cataloging-in-Publication Data
is available from the Library of Congress.

Photographs and illustrations are listed by
source and page number under
Picture Credits on page 189.

TABLE OF CONTENTS

Artemis I Space Launch System (SLS) and *Orion* spacecraft, atop the mobile launcher, in advance of launch from pad 39B at Kennedy Space Center in Florida on June 14, 2022, with a full moon in view.

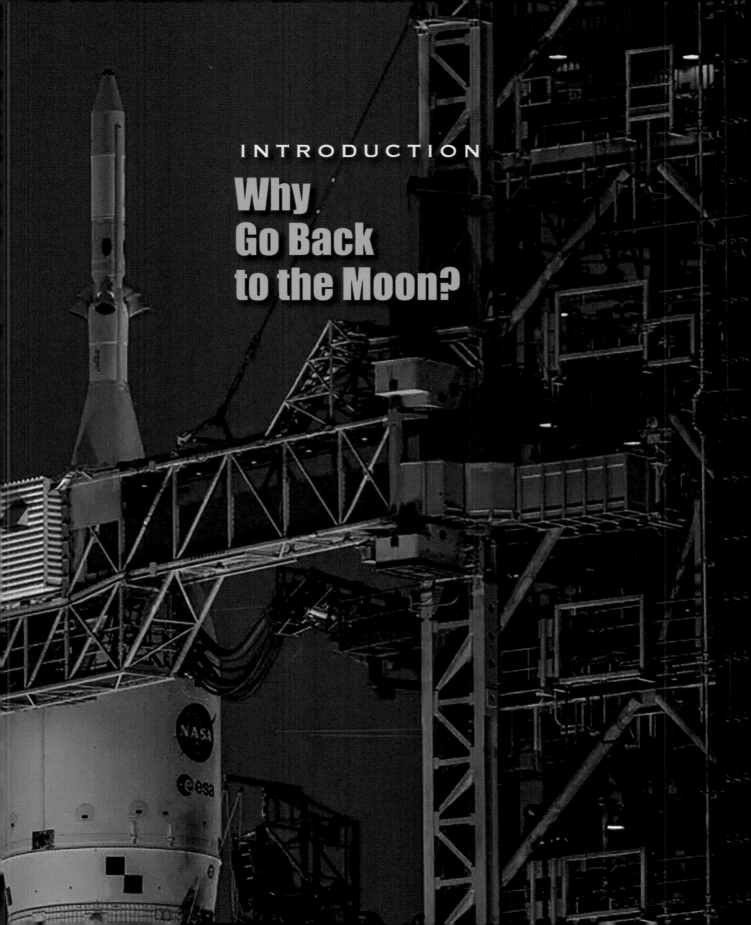

Why Go Back to the Moon?

White clouds streaked across the bright blue sky over the Pacific Ocean near Baja California. It was a beautiful day to be on the water. Yet all eyes aboard the USS *Portland*, a Navy amphibious transport dock ship, were trained on the sky. Today, history was about to be made.

Engineers at the Johnson Space Center, in Houston, Texas, were on alert. The *Orion* spacecraft, launched as part of the Artemis I mission, was coming home. Its safe landing was the final step in a successful mission around the Moon.

The engineers watched their video screens, closely monitoring *Orion*'s reentry. The spacecraft was subjected to temperatures of 5,000 degrees Fahrenheit during reentry into the atmosphere. That's half as hot as the Sun. But the spacecraft itself was protected from harm. Its specially designed heat shield kept *Orion* and its contents safe.

About thirty minutes before splashdown, *Orion* entered Earth's atmosphere. Traveling at a speed of over 25,000 miles per hour, it appeared as a blaze of fire. At 26,500 feet, the first three parachutes deployed. *Orion* would need eight more special parachutes, deployed at specific altitudes, to slow the speed of its descent to 20 mph before it could splash in the ocean. So far, everything was working according to plan.

The engineers from NASA's Exploration Ground Systems stood on the deck

Orion descending toward the Pacific Ocean with parachutes deployed.

of the *Portland* looking up. Squinting a bit, they pointed toward the sky.

There it was.

Orion!

NASA's three signature orange-and-white striped main parachutes billowed above the spacecraft, slowing its descent to allow for a soft landing. Navy personnel and NASA engineers on the ship, as well as NASA personnel at the Johnson Space Center, eagerly watched as *Orion* descended gracefully into the ocean.

Splashdown!

Thousands of people around the world watching the live-streamed video cheered—none louder than the multitude of engineers, technicians, scientists, and others who had worked so hard for more than ten years to make this accomplishment a reality. They had done it.

Artemis completed its first mission at 9:40 a.m. Pacific Standard Time on December 11, 2022. This flight occurred fifty years after Apollo 17, NASA's last mission to the Moon, landed on the lunar surface in 1972. Its success would pave a path back to that same lunar surface. The Moon was in reach for NASA once again.

"This is an extraordinary day," said NASA Administrator Bill Nelson. "It's historic, because we are now going back into space—deep space—with a new generation."

"We choose to go to the Moon in this decade and do the other things, not because they are easy, but because they are hard," President Kennedy told the crowd at Rice University in Houston.

September 12, 1962

Why are we going back to the Moon now? To answer this question, we will look into the past to see when the first seeds of space exploration were planted.

A Look Back

On September 12, 1962, President John F. Kennedy gave his most famous speech about space. "We choose to go to the Moon," he said. Those seven words ignited a race between the United States and its biggest rival at the time, the Soviet Union, to reach the farthest point in the universe that humans had ever dared to visit—the Moon.

Given the incentive, the technology, and the funding to make this happen, America's space agency, the National Aeronautics and Space Administration (NASA), succeeded. Between July 1969 and December 1972, twelve men, all Americans, walked on the lunar surface and returned to Earth.

But after twelve trips, the agency stopped sending astronauts there. Why? NASA decided to focus instead on building an international space station to maintain a human presence in space. To achieve this aim, it collaborated with the Japanese, Canadians, and even Russians, the very people the United States had competed with in the first place. The ultimate result was the International Space Station, the ISS, which has been in service since 2000. A multinational effort, the ISS has successfully allowed NASA to focus on learning to live and work in low Earth orbit (LEO), an area of outer space just above the Earth, for more than two decades.

Orion with its heat shield facing Earth as it encounters the denser atmosphere around the planet (artist's rendering).

A Look Forward

Now more than fifty years later, the US is determined to return to the Moon. And America is not the only country itching to go—China, Russia, and other countries are, too. NASA's reason for wanting to go back involves several objectives. One is that NASA would like to land the first woman and first person of color on the lunar surface. It also wishes to build a base to establish a long-term presence on the Moon. This base would be used as a jumping-off point for exploring deep space.

Finally, once a base is established, engineers and scientists could explore the Moon to learn more about its resources. There is evidence that the Moon has water, possibly in the form of ice mixed with the lunar surface, a layer of rock and dust called regolith.

Helium-3 is another valuable resource that could help engineers develop energy for nuclear fusion—a reaction that powers the sun and stars—for future use in space and on Earth. Both of these resources would make it easier for humans to establish a long-term presence on the Moon.

By living and working on the lunar surface, scientists could also study the Moon up close—its geography, gravity, and subsurface properties, which could help us better understand Earth and other planets in our solar system.

Getting Along in Outer Space

Accomplishing these feats would mean building habitats, laboratories, machines, and more in an airless, dust-covered, low-gravity environment. Challenges like these can be exhilarating but are not easy. This is especially true when multiple countries and companies are involved. Every person or country could have a different opinion about how things should work.

For example, what if two countries want to build in the same location on the Moon? Or what if there isn't enough water for everyone? Who will resolve conflicts that arise, or set guidelines for humans living in space?

When people live and work together, it's a good idea to have rules or guidelines to help them make decisions and get along with each other.

Are there laws for space, the Moon, and other celestial bodies? The answer is yes . . . but there are complications. Here's the background.

The first international law for space was the Outer Space Treaty (OST), which members of the United Nations drafted in 1967. The OST laid out broad principles for international cooperation in space. Principles are beliefs or values you support, like being honest and kind to other people. One of the most important principles in the OST says that "the exploration and use of outer space, including the Moon and other celestial bodies . . . shall be the province of all mankind." (Many UN documents from this period refer to "mankind." We prefer the broader term "humankind.")

In other words, the ability to explore space should be available to everyone—no matter who you are or where you live. The OST was—and is—a monumental achievement, and so far, 112 countries have signed it. So, what's the problem?

Treaties are law. They are meant to be obeyed. Yet they are open to different interpretations and can be tricky to enforce. They also need to be reviewed over time because situations change. Given the intense interest and activity in space today, it has become apparent that the OST has gaps that no one thought about in 1967. For instance, it did not occur to anyone then—except science fiction writers—that private citizens would be touring in space. And the creators of the OST could never have predicted the number of satellites currently orbiting our planet.

The UN has developed four more space agreements that are beginning

NASA's *Orion* spacecraft splashed down in the Pacific Ocean on December 11, 2022, after a 25.5-day mission to the Moon.

to fill some gaps. These too, though, leave questions about what will happen if people disagree with each other in space or on the Moon.

Basically, the world needs updated "rules of the road" to ensure that we work together peacefully in space. Developing these rules and encouraging countries—and companies—to accept them is a big task. It's about as big as getting to and living on the Moon!

This book will show you some of the technologies that are taking us back to the Moon, as well as how humans might manage themselves while on the surface, again. We'll also describe steps you can take to get involved!

But first, looking at how we got to this point is a useful way to understand where we are going. Let's head back to the 1950s, where the very first steps of our journey to the Moon began.

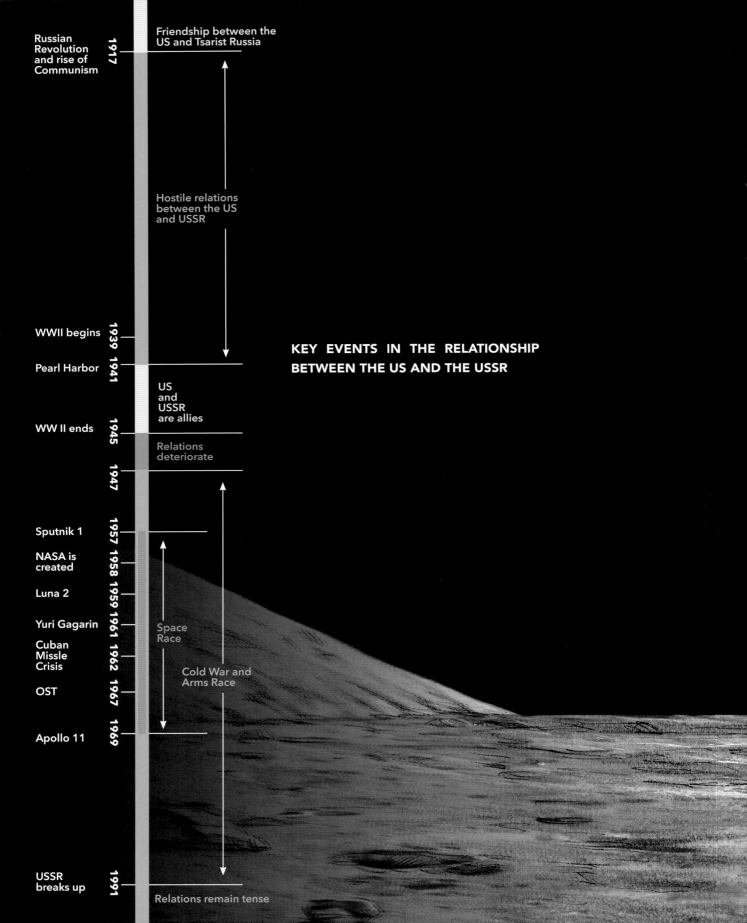

KEY EVENTS IN THE RELATIONSHIP BETWEEN THE US AND THE USSR

1917 — Russian Revolution and rise of Communism

Friendship between the US and Tsarist Russia

Hostile relations between the US and USSR

1939 — WWII begins
1941 — Pearl Harbor

US and USSR are allies

1945 — WW II ends

Relations deteriorate

1947

1957 — Sputnik 1
1958 — NASA is created
1959 — Luna 2
1961 — Yuri Gagarin
1962 — Cuban Missle Crisis
1967 — OST
1969 — Apollo 11

Space Race

Cold War and Arms Race

1991 — USSR breaks up

Relations remain tense

CHAPTER 1

Flags on the Moon

EXPLORING HISTORY

Three forces were rattling Americans in the 1950s and 1960s—a cold war, an arms race, and a space race. It appeared that the first two might lead to the total destruction of the world as everyone knew it. The third—the space race—promised exciting opportunities for discovering new worlds.

All three involved the Soviet Union. And they ramped up when the Soviets landed Luna 2 on the Moon.

"Reds' 'Lunik' Hits the Moon"

It's mid-September 1959. Kids across America have just shelled out about seventy cents for the Saturday matinee at their local movie theater, maybe to catch another showing of *The Shaggy Dog*. Settled in their seats in the darkened theater with their bags of popcorn, they wait for the feature film to start—or, if they're lucky, a double feature. But before the film begins, they might get a double dose of space.

First up: *Space Mouse*, Universal Studios' new cartoon. Doc, a Siamese cat wearing a top hat, reads that a Missile Test Center needs more mice. Without them, the missile race might be lost! Doc tries to capture two mice named Hickory and Dickory so they can be shot into space. But they outwit him, of course.

Then—whoa!—the whole audience leans back in their seats, gaping at the Universal Studios newsreel. A rumbling roar and raucous patriotic music blare as on the screen a rocket, billowing smoke, lifts straight up from a launch pad. In the next two minutes, the rocket breaks through Earth's cloud cover and appears to keep on climbing. Where is it heading?

The voice-over of announcer Ed Herlihy urgently explains: "Soviet Russia scores a dramatic victory in the exploration of space with the launching of the first rocket to hit the Moon!" Not only that, but the rocket carried a payload—an 858-pound, baseball-size sphere Herlihy dubs "Lunik." "Bearing the Soviet coat of arms and hammer-and-sickle pennants," he goes on, "it traveled thirty-five hours through space. It is the first man-made object to voyage from one cosmic body to another." Riveted by the newsreel, kids learn that Luna 2 sliced through roughly 240,000 miles of outer space and hit the Moon "almost dead on target." How exciting!

But then the announcer explains that the feat gives a "propaganda bonus to Khrushchev on the eve of his visit to America." Wait. Khrushchev, the leader of the Soviet government, is in the United States, and he's getting a public-relations boost while he's here? Isn't the Soviet Union our enemy?

Tonight, kids will have a lot to dream about—along with perhaps a few nightmares.

Scan the QR code to view the Universal Studios newsreel and *Space Mouse* cartoon.

Frigid Former Friends

The United States and Russia have had a long, complicated relationship—first friendly, then tense, sometimes both at once. You might be surprised to learn that the daughter of a former US president, John Quincy Adams, was born—and is buried—there. Louisa Adams was born in 1812, while her father was serving as the first Minister Plenipotentiary to the Russian Empire. Sadly, she died there the next year.

Relations between the two countries remained amicable as long as a tsar ruled Russia. Americans can thank Tsar Alexander II for selling off Alaska in 1867 for a mere two cents an acre. Connections vanished, however, following the Russian Revolution in 1917. That's when the tsars met their end, and the new leadership soon turned communist and called for worldwide revolution. At that point, the US refused to recognize the Russian government for many years and even tried to undermine it.

That hostility abruptly ended, for a while, two years after the start of World War II. In June 1941, Nazi Germany invaded the Soviet Union. The USSR was taken completely by surprise because the two countries had signed a treaty when the war began promising to leave each other alone. Nazi soldiers were so successful it looked as if they might take over the entire Soviet Union the way they seemed to be overrunning Europe.

For the next six months, the United States stayed out of the war. However,

SOVIET UNION

Russia? Soviet Union?

From 1922 to 1991, the Union of Soviet Socialist Republics was a nation composed of multiple republics. The most powerful republic was Russia. The entire territory was so vast it stretched across eleven time zones. Called the USSR (CCCP in Russian), the Soviet Union, or Soviet Russia, all of it was ruled by the Communist Party, which was headquartered at the Kremlin in Moscow. We use these terms when talking about the region during that period. Otherwise, we refer to it as Russia.

on December 7, 1941, the Japanese bombed Pearl Harbor, America's naval base in Hawaii. The very next day, the US declared war on Japan, and soon Germany declared war on America. The US immediately joined the Allies, which included the Soviets, to defeat the Axis powers.

This alliance, however, was very short-lived. Almost as soon as the war ended in 1945, the two countries went back to following very different paths. The United States remained a democracy, with leadership elected by voters. The Soviet Union remained a totalitarian system, led by a dictator who had total control over everything—politics, culture, agriculture, work, and more. Americans believed in capitalism: people could own and run their own businesses. Soviets believed in communism: the government owns practically everything and decides who gets what.

The United States and the Soviet Union were the two most powerful countries on the globe, and they viewed the world very differently. Each believed that its own political and economic system was the best, not only for its own citizens but for everyone everywhere. And it appeared that both countries were willing to act to ensure their system won.

The enduring question was, Would democracy or communism dominate the world? And the ongoing fear was, Would it take another war for the outcome to be decided?

Tensions were so high that some Americans dug bunkers underneath their yards. They lined them with concrete and filled them with canned food in the event that the Soviets launched a nuclear attack. Children practiced "duck and cover" drills under their school desks, which they were told, wrongly, would protect them from a nuclear blast. Some especially fearful people even opposed adding fluoride to the water supply, which is good for children's teeth, because they claimed it was a communist plot. Both Americans and Soviets posted double and triple agents to spy on each other.

This was how the Cold War was playing out.

FALLOUT SHELTER

This version of the national fallout shelter sign was introduced to the public by the US Defense Department on December 1, 1961, as part of civil defense preparations in the event of a nuclear attack. By the late 1970s, the fallout shelter program was discontinued.

Entrance to an underground fallout shelter on Long Island, New York, 1955.

No bombs, missiles, or rockets flying through the air, but rampant mistrust on both sides as the superpowers vied for global dominance. "Cold War" was an apt description.

To Arms!

Though this mutual hostility was considered a "cold" war, it still involved arms—and an arms race. For a few years, Americans thought they were ahead and would stay there because no one else had atomic weaponry. General Leslie Groves, who directed the Manhattan Project, which developed the atom bomb unleashed on Hiroshima and Nagasaki, assured them of that. In 1945, he stated that the Soviets couldn't catch up for at least another twenty years. Yet just four years later they trumpeted their own nuclear explosion.

Americans panicked and the Soviets felt triumphant, especially as communism continued to spread to China and then North Korea. Would the United States or one of its democratic allies be the next to fall?

From 1947 to 1992, the two superpowers stockpiled enough nuclear and other weapons to annihilate much of the populations of both countries and possibly life on Earth. By the early 1950s, each side had not only atomic bombs but also hydrogen "super bombs." In 1957, the Soviets successfully tested an intercontinental ballistic missile (ICBM). The term "intercontinental" means that their missiles could travel more than 3,500 miles. This would allow them to cross the Atlantic or Pacific Ocean and detonate in America. The US soon followed with its own ICBM tests. The real concern was whether either side would stop at tests.

The arms race reached a peak in 1962 when the USSR moved some of its nuclear missiles to Cuba, just 90 miles south of Florida—and within easy bombing distance of Washington, DC. After all, Soviet Premier Nikita Khrushchev reasoned, the US had placed its missiles in Turkey, along the USSR's border, three years earlier and had shown no signs of moving them. Placing Soviet missiles off America's coastline was just payback, or so the USSR believed.

For thirteen harrowing days in 1962, both sides scrambled jets, submarines, and warships. President John F. Kennedy ordered a naval blockade around Cuba. If the Soviets tried to break through, the US had plans to retaliate with nuclear arms. The intensity of this mounting crisis was felt not just in the US; a feeling of doom settled over people around the world.

Unbeknownst to most people, Kennedy and Khrushchev used a teletype machine to send encrypted messages back and forth throughout the crisis.

From these exchanges it is clear that neither side wanted to be the one to order an attack. Fortunately, they came to an agreement. The Soviets would dismantle their missiles. The Americans would not invade Cuba, and they would remove their missiles from Turkey. The world breathed a sigh of relief. The crisis was over.

Yet each of the superpowers still possessed a vast number of weapons. It would be another twenty-five years before the threat of world annihilation was eased, a bit.

The US and USSR established a hotline for use during the Cuban Missile Crisis. They chose to communicate via a teleprinter, not a telephone, reasoning that print was the best way to send very clear messages.

On October 4, 1957, the USSR successfully launched Sputnik I, the world's first artificial satellite that was about the size of a beach ball. It marked the start of the Space Age. Also shown is a commemorative Soviet stamp, one of many items the USSR created to celebrate Sputnik.

And Now an Arms Race in Space, Too?

The tit-for-tat arms buildups and escalating threats between the superpowers were frightening enough on Earth. In 1957—five years before the Cuban missile crisis and two years before Luna 2 hit the Moon—events turned truly alarming for the US. The Cold War and, possibly, the arms race took a big leap . . . into space.

That was the year the USSR launched Sputnik (Russian for "traveling companion"), the first satellite to successfully orbit the Earth. The rest of the world, including American leadership, was caught completely off guard. What was the satellite up to?

For three months, until its batteries failed, people listening over a short-wave radio could hear Sputnik beep ominously. Many people could see it, even without binoculars, in the early morning or late afternoon as it passed overhead.

Sputnik's presence was a constant reminder of the USSR's technical know-how. The Soviets' engineering ability was far above anything that any other country, even the US, had at that moment. This was deeply concerning to America and other democratic countries.

While everyone wondered if the USSR was going to use its new space satellite as a weapon, the Soviets actually had other—grander—ideas. They wanted to put a human into space. To test whether it was possible to keep a living being alive in space, they launched a dog, Laika, into orbit on Sputnik 2, just one month after Sputnik 1. The dog, sadly, died a short time after launch, but the Soviets were determined to keep going.

Unfortunately, the US was nowhere near ready to launch anything into space. In fact, the country's very next attempt, a Vanguard rocket, exploded on the pad at Cape Canaveral, Florida, on December 6, 1957. To help the US on its own path, President Dwight David Eisenhower urged Congress to create the National Aeronautics and Space Administration (NASA). Congress agreed, and in 1958—just ten months after Sputnik 1—the space race was on!

The Soviet Union set its sights on the Moon. It wanted to be the first country to land an object on the lunar surface. On September 14, 1959, the Luna 2 spacecraft crashed mere feet from its target near the Sea of Serenity.

Its metal sphere flew apart on impact, scattering seventy-two pennants,

A replica of Luna 2, the spherical Soviet spacecraft that was the first craft to land on the Moon.

Pick One: Diplomacy or War?

Eisenhower welcomed Khrushchev with a twenty-one-gun salute and hosted a state dinner for the visitor, who then toured America for twelve days. If the United States and the Soviet Union were spying on each other and accumulating massive stockpiles of weapons, why was the president of the US acting chummy with the premier of the USSR?

Both leaders realized that unless they sat down and talked together, the two superpowers were inevitably headed toward World War III. Their negotiations over disarmament, trade, and cultural exchanges during the last two weeks of September 1959 didn't resolve the Cold War or the space race. But they did avert a nuclear war, which, Eisenhower reminded Khrushchev, would amount to "mutual suicide."

President Eisenhower holding a gift from Soviet Premier Nikita Khrushchev, a replica of the metal ball launched to the lunar surface from within Luna 2.

inscribed with the hammer-and-sickle insignia of that "Red" communist country, across the surface of the Moon. With this spacecraft's Moon landing, the Soviets symbolically threw down the challenge flag. They implied that space and the Moon were up for grabs.

In an announcement to celebrate this success, Khrushchev hinted that the Soviet Union had just taken possession of that celestial body. The day after Luna 2 landed, Khrushchev took part in a ceremony in the Oval Office. He grinned while handing a replica of Luna 2 to President Eisenhower. Did Khrushchev's gleeful grin suggest something ominous?

A few weeks later he boasted, "Americans sleep under a Soviet Moon."

People around the world were frightened by the idea of looking up every night at a Moon that might one day be controlled by communists. American officials tried to sound reassuring. Just because the Soviet Union had flung its pennants around the Moon did not mean that the Kremlin ruled that celestial body. According to the *New York Times*, a spokesman for the US State Department said that "the Soviet Union would have to do considerably more than 'stick a Red flag in the ground' to establish moon sovereignty."

Soviet pennants bearing the hammer-and-sickle symbol of the USSR. Luna 2 scattered pennants like these on the Moon.

Kidnapping Luna

It wasn't just American and Soviet politicians who were highly suspicious of each other. So were ordinary citizens.

To reduce tensions and help people in both countries understand each other's societies, Eisenhower and Khrushchev agreed to sponsor cultural exchanges. In addition to ballet dancers visiting each other's home turf, the Soviets sent mock-ups of Luna 2 on a tour around the United States. Except, oops, one of them wasn't a mock-up. The engine and most of its electronics had been removed, but it still contained lots of valuable components. And the Central Intelligence Agency (CIA), America's major spy organization, realized that. So of course, they concocted a plan to "borrow" and investigate it.

One night, CIA agents followed the truck transporting this Luna. After the driver went to his hotel, the agents drove the truck to a secure lot and went to work. They carefully opened the crate and climbed in. There was the "payload orb"—a metal globe decorated with pennants, like the one Khrushchev handed Eisenhower—complete with its antennas. They also found fuel tanks, wiring, and other hardware, all of which they photographed in detail.

Finally, the agents meticulously tidied up, making sure not to leave stray screwdrivers or bolts, reassembled the crate, and returned the truck to the hotel. Mission accomplished. No one was the wiser—no Soviets, that is. Just some American spies, who had learned where and how Luna 2 was built.

This CIA secret report on Luna 2 was declassified in 2019.

SECRET
NO FOREIGN DISSEM

STUDIES in INTELLIGENCE

SECRET

The Lunik

found that it was indeed a production item from which the engine and most electrical and electronic components had been removed. They examined it thoroughly from the viewpoint of probable performance, taking measurements, determining its structural characteristics and wiring format, estimating engine size, and so forth.[1]

Now one of the things intelligence can do, and routinely does, with a piece of important Soviet hardware is to identify the plants that manufactured it and its components through detailed analysis of the factory markings stamped or stenciled on them.[2] A few markings had been copied from the Lunik during this operation, but not with sufficient detail or precision to permit a definitive identification of the producer or determination of the markings system used. It was therefore decided to try to get another access for a factory markings team.

[1] For the ultimate contribution of this information and a sketch of the Lunik see "Intelligence for the Space Race," by Albert D. Wheelon and Sidney N. Graybeal, in *Studies* V 4, p. 1 ff, in particular pp. 9-11.

34

SECRET

"Это мое!"
(Translation: "That's mine!")

What would it take for a country to stake a claim to an entire celestial body—and convince other countries to say, "Sure. Take it. That one's yours." Could a government own the Moon just because it was the first to smash a pennant-bearing rocket onto the surface?

Power grabs have existed throughout history. For instance, in 1492, Spanish and Portuguese explorers staked their flags in the Americas, effectively claiming them. Five years later, in 1497, John Cabot explored the coast of North America and, not seeing anyone, he handed possession of that landmass over to King Henry VII of England. By the 1700s, Great Britain established thirteen colonies there. And in 1939, only twenty years before Luna 2 crash-landed on the Moon, Nazi troops marched their swastika-emblazoned flag into Poland and then a succession of other countries, claiming them for the German Fatherland.

Was the Space Age going to be like the Age of Discovery, more than four hundred years earlier? That was when European nations began exploring the world, and when planting a flag someplace meant controlling vast terrain and creating outposts. In 1959, the answer to this question wasn't clear. So why did the USSR lob its national symbols onto the Moon? The answer probably had less to do with ownership or sovereignty than with bragging rights.

Soviet poster conveying a statement about the USSR's dominance in space.

The United Nations Weighs In

The US didn't agree that the Moon was Soviet, and much of the world *hoped* it wasn't so. People around the globe gaped at films of the USSR's successful launches, fearing what this superpower might do next. Because so many countries expressed concern, the United Nations took action.

Three months after Luna 2 crash-landed, the UN created a Committee on the Peaceful Uses of Outer Space (COPUOS). Membership consisted of two dozen nations, ranging from Albania to the United States—but not the Soviet Union, which boycotted it for a few years.

The Committee's purpose was—and remains—to ensure that

- "the exploration and use of outer space [is] for the betterment" of humankind,
- the "extension of present national rivalries into this new field" is avoided, and
- "international cooperation in . . . outer space for peaceful purposes" is encouraged.

The importance of these principles hit home a few years later when Soviet cosmonaut Yuri Gagarin became the first human to reach space. The Soviets had maintained their edge in the space race. Had the US lost? Not yet. The US saw the USSR's achievement as a challenge. It would work harder to accomplish something far more significant.

What *Is* the United Nations?

The United Nations was created in October 1945, just after the end of World War II, and is composed of 193 member countries. Meeting at its headquarters in New York City, members discuss and vote on issues and carry out programs regarding international relations, human rights, worldwide health, and other concerns.

The UN is composed of several parts, including the following:

- The UN General Assembly, which includes every country. This body discusses and adopts resolutions and treaties. Treaties are like laws; they are legally binding agreements between countries.
- The Security Council, which focuses on peace and security. It consists of the United Kingdom, China, France, Russia, and the US, as well as ten rotating members. Unlike the General Assembly, the Security Council can enforce its decisions by punishing countries economically or sending UN soldiers to battle zones.
- The International Court of Justice, which deals with cases that nations bring against other nations.

KEY EVENTS IN THE SPACE RACE

■ US

■ Soviet Union (until 1991) / Russia

PROJECT MERCURY

PROJECT GEMINI

APOLLO MOON LANDINGS

SKYLAB TESTS LIVING IN SPACE

Shepard achieves suborbital flight

JFK speaks at Rice

Cooper completes 22 orbits

June 3, White walks in space

OST

Apollo 11

1958   1961   1962   1963   1964   1965   1966   1967   1968   1969   1972   1973   1975   1979

Gagarin orbits Earth

March 18, Lenov walks in space

Apollo-Soyuz partnership

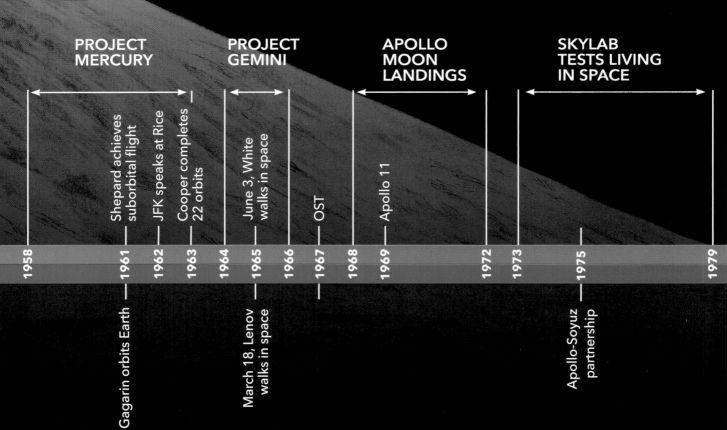

CHAPTER 2

Seeking a Lunar Perspective

A RACE TO PUT HUMANS ON THE MOON

In 1962, tensions between the US and the Soviet Union were rapidly escalating. US citizens were on alert. They feared that a confrontation between the two superpowers might be imminent. What everyone needed was a positive distraction. Something. Anything. It might perhaps be in the form of a rallying cry that would unite the country. On a warm September day in Houston, Texas, President John F. Kennedy provided just that.

1986

2001

MIR SPACE
STATION

"We Choose to Go to the Moon"

It was September 12, 1962. President John F. Kennedy had spent the last two days touring the Manned Spacecraft Center (now Johnson Space Center) in Houston. Before he left, the president wanted to give a speech. He chose the football stadium of Rice University as his venue.

Since the students weren't back in classes yet, the public was invited. The stadium was full of schoolchildren, teenagers, local citizens, and of course, professors from the university.

Rodney Griffin, a high schooler at the time, remembers that "[a] group of us boarded the yellow school bus and came across town."

Charles Helpinstill, a Rice University alumnus, recalled: "I clearly remember that bright, beautiful day. All of us were dressed in white short-sleeve shirts with skinny ties."

It seemed like a great day to come hear the young, dynamic leader speak. A huge roar went up! The President's limousine had entered the end zone. JFK sat proudly in the back, smiling and waving to the crowd as he passed in front of the packed seats.

A few minutes later, President Kennedy stepped to the podium, his engaging grin on display. He began his speech by complimenting the city, the school, and the state of Texas.

"We meet at a college noted for knowledge, in a city noted for progress, in a state noted for strength, and we stand in need of all three, for we meet in an hour of change and challenge, in a decade of hope and fear, in an age of both knowledge and ignorance," Kennedy said.

The President was building toward something spectacular, and the crowd knew it. They hung on his every word. Kennedy's rousing speech celebrated the explorers of the past and encouraged the nation to consider a new place to explore, one that surprised them all.

"We choose to go to the Moon. We choose to go to the Moon in this decade and do the other things, not because they are easy, but because they are hard, because that goal will serve to organize and measure the best of our energies and skills, because

President John F. Kennedy delivers a rousing speech at Rice University on the nation's space effort.

that challenge is one that we are willing to accept, one we are unwilling to postpone, and one which we intend to win."

The crowd erupted in deafening cheers! They were behind him one hundred percent.

His speech was broadcast across the country. That day, President Kennedy inspired a nation to look to the skies, see the Moon, and, finally, to imagine an American walking upon it.

President Kennedy's inspiring address at Rice University put the world on notice. The United States intended not only to be the first nation to put a person on the Moon but also to do it by the end of the decade.

At the time, the US did not possess the technology to get into space, let alone to the Moon. Every piece of equipment—from the spacecraft to the rocket to the very suits the astronauts would wear—had to be created from scratch. The task President Kennedy had set forth seemed impossible. For NASA and its teams of amazing engineers and scientists, it was an exciting new challenge, one they approached with great urgency.

With direct support from the President and Congress, NASA ramped up Project Mercury, which was the US's first step toward putting a human into space. Its mission goals were to

- launch a piloted spacecraft into orbit around the Earth,
- understand what it would take to keep a human alive in space, and
- bring humans safely back to Earth.

As NASA was working furiously to meet President Kennedy's directive, the Soviets were set on achieving similar goals. On April 12, 1961, they were the first to launch a spacecraft containing

What Does It Mean to Orbit Earth?

An orbit is the regular, consistent path one object takes around another object in space. For example, the Moon is said to orbit Earth because every twenty-seven days, seven hours, and forty-three minutes it completes one full trip, or revolution, around the planet. It also travels the same path every time. Orbits are typically elliptical in shape, which means that the object travels in an oval path. An object that orbits another is called a satellite. There are natural satellites, like the Moon, and man-made satellites.

Satellites and spacecraft need to maintain a specific velocity in order to stay in orbit. Objects that cannot maintain that speed are said to be on a suborbital path. Suborbital flights are ones where the craft may circle the Earth but cannot stay in that same path because gravity pulls it down. An airplane or craft that is unable to reach the speed of 17,500 mph cannot maintain orbit.

Put simply, suborbital flights are a first step to understanding what is required to achieve a consistent orbit around the Earth.

a human into space when cosmonaut Yuri Gagarin made a 108-minute orbital flight around the Earth.

But the US was not out of the race yet. In May 1961, twenty-three days after Gagarin's flight, NASA launched the Mercury-Redstone 3 mission, commonly called Freedom 7. Aboard the mission's spacecraft, also called *Freedom 7*, was Navy test pilot and astronaut Alan B. Shepard Jr., who became the first American to achieve suborbital spaceflight.

During the flight, *Freedom 7* reached a height of 116 miles (187 km), a point which was technically in outer space. But Shepard's spacecraft was not powerful enough to maintain that height for very long because it could only go 5,134 mph—not the 17,500 mph required for a craft to stay in orbit. Still, Shepard stayed aloft for fifteen minutes and then splashed down safely in the Atlantic Ocean. NASA had fulfilled its mission. By putting an astronaut into space, it was one step closer to landing on the Moon. Look out, USSR, the US was gaining ground in the space race!

NASA quickly followed the success of Mercury-Redstone 3 with five more missions. The last one was Mercury-Atlas 9 launched in May 1963. Air Force pilot and astronaut Gordon Cooper completed twenty-two orbits of the Earth in just over 34 hours.

The US was making its mark in space, yet the Soviets continued to stay just slightly ahead. On March 18, 1965, cosmonaut Alexei Lenov became the first person to walk in space—a feat the US was not even close to accomplishing. It appeared that the US might forever remain behind the Soviets in the race to reach the Moon.

NASA was not about to give up. Not when its progress was just starting to gain momentum. Using all the accumulated experience learned from the Mercury missions, NASA began Project Gemini.

During this time, Gemini astronauts broke records for

- the longest time spent in space (nearly 14 days during Gemini 7),
- the first to dock with another vehicle in space (Gemini 9), and
- the first to conduct three spacewalks, totaling five and a half hours (Gemini 4 and others).

Throughout both the Mercury and Gemini missions, NASA focused on making bigger, stronger, more technologically advanced rockets and capsules. The goal? A safe landing of the first American on the Moon.

VEHICLES FOR MANNED SPACE FLIGHT

Launch vehicles designed for NASA space flight programs from 1960 to 1973. Notice that the rockets increased in size to meet the requirements of landing on the Moon during the Apollo missions.

| REDSTONE MERCURY | ATLAS MERCURY | TITAN II | SATURN I | SATURN IB | SATURN V |

The Outer Space Treaty: Space Is the "Province of All Mankind"

While NASA was working hard to create the technology to get to the Moon, people around the world were still concerned that the arms race would spill over into space. President Kennedy tried to reassure everyone, saying, "We shall not see it governed by a hostile flag of conquest, but by a banner of freedom and peace."

Tragically, President Kennedy was as-sassinated in 1963, but the next president, Lyndon B. Johnson, vowed to carry out Kennedy's aim. Even though the USSR and the US still had frosty relations, in 1966 he dispatched Arthur Goldberg, America's ambassador to the UN, to work with Nikolai Fedorenko, the Soviet representative to the UN.

Goldberg and Fedorenko put their heads together to develop guidelines for spacefaring nations. There was plenty of discord as they and other members of the UN's Committee on the Peaceful Uses of Outer Space negotiated a variety of questions. For instance, could countries inspect each other's installations once they were established on the Moon? Should countries share what they learn with other nations? What about those that could not afford to send missions to space? Liberia's president, William V. S. Tubman, reminded the wealthy countries that "no matter how small, no matter how struggling, no matter how poor we may be, we share the same heavens with the greatest Powers."

After COPUOS members made a series of compromises, the UN in 1967 adopted the Treaty on Principles Governing the Activities of States in the Exploration and Use of Outer Space, including the Moon and Other Celestial Bodies. This mouthful of a title was quickly nicknamed the Outer Space Treaty, or OST.

Some people call the OST the Magna Carta of space. That's because it provides the basis for deciding the rights and responsibilities of countries in the space domain. You might think of the OST as being like the American Declaration of Independence because it expresses fundamental values and beliefs. And like the Declaration, which required a constitution to bring it to life, the OST

has led to four other treaties. You'll read about these in later chapters.

The first principle in the OST states that exploring and using space should be for the good of everyone. The second one says that no one can own any of it.

Article I
The exploration and use of outer space . . . shall be carried out for the benefit . . . of all countries . . . and shall be the province of all [hu]mankind.

Article II
Outer space, including the moon and other celestial bodies, is not subject to national appropriation by claim of sovereignty, by means of use or occupation, or by any other means.

Since nuclear arms were on everyone's minds, people were vastly relieved to see that the Outer Space Treaty also said that no nuclear weapons can orbit Earth or be put on celestial bodies.

Article IV
States . . . undertake not to place in orbit around the earth any objects carrying nuclear weapons or any other kinds of weapons of mass destruction, install such weapons on celestial bodies, or station such weapons in outer space in any other manner.

There were a couple of wrinkles. For instance, the OST still allowed nuclear weapons to travel *through* space. But most earthlings felt safe from being bombarded from above.

Above all, the OST emphasized that space must remain peaceful.

> **Article IV**
> *The moon and other celestial bodies shall be used . . . exclusively for peaceful purposes.*

Treaty-signing ceremonies took place at the White House, London, and Moscow in January 1967, and the treaty went into effect in October, a week after the tenth anniversary of the launching of the first Sputnik. President Johnson hailed the accord, saying, "Space is a frontier that is common to all mankind and it should be explored and conquered by humanity acting in concert." The Soviet Union's ambassador, Anatoly P. Dobrynin, added that "the treaty . . . will be an important step in further development of cooperation and understanding among states and peoples." Two dozen ambassadors then affixed their signatures.

This was a monumental achievement. With this treaty, space and the bodies in it became enshrined as "the province of all" humankind, free for exploration and use by all. And the world's two major rivals came together to declare it so.

One Giant Leap for Mankind

With just three years left until the end of the decade, NASA began its boldest effort yet: Project Apollo. Its goals were to

- build the technology that would allow the US to land humans on the Moon,
- establish the US as a superior presence in space,
- carry out scientific research on the Moon, and
- learn how humans can live and work on the Moon.

The US set the goal to be the first country to land a human on the Moon. While not all of that happened with Project Apollo, it was a bold undertaking that would require huge amounts of work—the creation of a spacecraft capable of reaching the Moon, landing humans there, and returning them safely to Earth. And the clock was ticking. . . .

NASA engineers worked at a feverish pace, and in July 1969, after tens of thousands of hours of work by over 400,000 men and women, the Apollo 11 mission to the Moon was ready. Astronauts Edwin "Buzz" Aldrin Jr., Neil Armstrong, and Michael Collins climbed into their spacecraft on pad 39A at Kennedy Space Center, strapped themselves in, and took off for the ride of a lifetime!

President Lyndon B. Johnson *(right)* watches the signing of the Outer Space Treaty at the White House with representatives from the USSR and the UK on January 27, 1967.

An American Flag on the Moon

On July 20, 1969, American astronauts landed and walked on the Moon. What was the first thing they did? They called home! Shortly after their lunar lander, named *Eagle*, settled into the powdery dust at the Sea of Tranquility, they spoke to some very relieved engineers at NASA in Houston. No one there was feeling tranquil, but Neil Armstrong and Buzz Aldrin sounded as cool as the Moon itself.

> *Eagle:* "Houston, Tranquility Base here. The Eagle has landed."
>
> *Houston:* "Roger, Tranquility, we copy you on the ground. You've got a bunch of guys about to turn blue. We're breathing again."
>
> *Eagle:* "A very smooth touchdown."

Aldrin and Armstrong spent the next four hours preparing for the biggest walk of their lives. Once the astronauts had ensured that the lander was safely in place, they donned their space suits and opened the door. They set the ladder into the lunar regolith. Then Armstrong climbed down the ladder and took the first step onto the lunar surface. He then said these now-famous words:

"That's one small step for [a] man, one giant leap for mankind."

Aldrin followed, and together the two planted an American flag on the surface of the Moon.

Later, when the astronauts were both safely back in the Apollo capsule, they spoke with President Richard M. Nixon. Armstrong told the President, "It's a great honor and privilege for us to be here representing not only the United States but men of peace of all nations."

Opposite: Iconic image of astronaut Buzz Aldrin saluting the American flag on the surface of the Moon during the Apollo 11 mission.

NASA had done it! Two humans successfully left footprints—and a flag—on another celestial body. To the United States, the Soviet Union, and the world, America had surged ahead in the space race.

The US wasn't about to stop there. It kept exploring the new lunar frontier. Between July 1969 and December 1972, twelve men, all Americans, walked on the Moon and returned safely to Earth. Astronauts conducted experiments in space, drove around in the lunar rover, and even hit a golf ball there. They also brought back samples of Moon dust and rocks for scientists to study. Much of what we know about the Moon today came from those first visits over fifty years ago.

Then the missions to the Moon ended.

The End of the Moon Trips

Why did the US stop going to the Moon? It was extremely expensive to keep going back to the Moon and landing humans there. After all, the rockets used to send the spacecraft into space were not reusable.

From the time President Kennedy made his bold pronouncement in 1962 until the return of the last astronaut in 1972, the Apollo program cost almost $24 billion. That's about $283 billion in today's money. Also, technology did not yet exist that would enable humans to stay on the Moon. Nor did NASA have any idea how to keep humans alive in space for a long time.

Heritage Sites on the Moon?

NASA considered sending flags of every country on Apollo 11 to make sure it didn't look like America was laying claim to the Moon. But that would have added too much weight. So, Neil Armstrong carried just the American flag. The one he left there was blown over by the rocket blast as the astronauts departed.

In addition to flags, hundreds of items deposited by five countries—so far—remain on the Moon, including cameras, tongs, nail clippers, and "defecation collection devices." Some scientists wonder if the Moon will need a dump site to collect the litter.

An organization called For All Moonkind has another idea. Historic areas, such as human lunar landing spots, should be preserved and recognized as Heritage Sites, the way the United Nations Educational, Scientific, and Cultural Organization (UNESCO) protects important places on Earth.

By 1972, even with all of the visits to the Moon, NASA only had the capability to send astronauts there, allow them to explore for a short time, then bring them back to Earth. While that was certainly an amazing feat, after sending twelve men there the novelty was starting to wear off. It was time to begin learning how to live in space for longer periods of time, and that wasn't going to happen on the Moon. It was too far away.

So the United States decided to focus on building a space station closer to home. That meant NASA also had to develop a reliable and reusable way to get to space and back.

In 1973, the US built and launched Skylab, the first American space station. It was not designed for astronauts to live there continuously. Instead, a crew of nine astronauts rotated through, living and working on Skylab on and off for a year. This was the first time that any American had spent a significant time in a microgravity environment. The experiences these astronauts went through and the knowledge gained were invaluable. This is the exact reason why NASA had turned its focus away from the Moon. Skylab was supposed to stay in orbit for eight to ten years. Unfortunately, in 1979 an unexpected solar storm caused it to fall out of orbit and burn up in the atmosphere upon reentry, five years after its last crew of astronauts left.

The US was not done living in space, though. Instead, it reached out a hand of friendship to another country.

To the surprise of many in the world, in 1975 the United States partnered with the USSR on the Apollo-Soyuz mission, the first joint space collaboration between the two countries. Why Soviet Russia? It was the only other country that had the technical knowledge to get to space. The collaboration during the Apollo-Soyuz mission would be the beginning of a very long space partnership.

Eleven years later, the Soviets built their Mir space station, which remained in space from 1986 to 2001. Mir was another collaboration between the two countries; both Russian cosmonauts and American astronauts lived and worked together there.

As Mir began to age, it was clear that a replacement space station was needed. In 1998, the United States began building the International Space Station (ISS) with an international team of partners, including Russia. The ISS was, and continues to be, a success. It has been in orbit around the Earth for more than two decades and is expected to remain in place until at least 2030.

Within the mostly aluminum and titanium walls of the ISS, enormous

How Far Away Is the Moon?

When you look up in the sky, the Moon may not seem that far away, but it's an average of 238,855 miles (384,400 km) from Earth. The Moon is also constantly drifting away from the Earth at about 1.5 inches (4 cm) per year, which means that every year that distance gets slightly larger.

The distance from the Earth to the Moon is so vast that every single planet in the solar system (including the dwarf planet Pluto) could fit into that space and still have about 1,305 miles (2,100 km) to spare.

amounts of knowledge have been gathered about the science, technology, and engineering required to keep humans alive in space. The research conducted on the ISS has been crucial to understanding how humans live within microgravity. All this is possible because the ISS is located in low Earth orbit, or LEO (discussed in detail in the next chapter), where experiments and their results are not bound by Earth's gravity. Much technology and information has been developed here on Earth because of the ISS.

Perhaps the most significant achievement of the ISS is that living in space is now literally a common, everyday activity. While it is still only for a select few at a time, having a space station this close to Earth makes it possible. With the huge advancements in technology developed on the ISS and the development of high-tech engineering on the Earth, the big question has remained: When will NASA head back to the Moon? The answer is . . . soon.

A Plan to Return

In 2005, with direction from President George W. Bush, NASA began the Constellation program to land a human on the Moon by 2020. As NASA worked to develop the technology needed for the return visit, vast expenditures resulted in major problems for the program. So, in January 2009, President Barack Obama shut down the Constellation program and canceled the Space Shuttle program. He then switched NASA's focus to landing on a near-Earth asteroid by 2025, and on Mars by the mid-2030s.

As you see, presidents set NASA's missions, priorities, and programs, and the head of NASA reports directly to the president. As a result, the space agency's focus can change abruptly every four or eight years when a new president takes office. And its funding can change every year when Congress adopts a new budget. That can make long-range planning for space a tricky undertaking.

But the Moon has always remained in NASA's sights. It is the nearest celestial body to Earth, and therefore the best place to learn to live and work for long periods of time—perhaps even years—in space. One of the main reasons the US is headed back to the Moon is that in 2019 President Donald Trump directed NASA to land humans there—this time, to stay.

Heading Back to the Moon

The Moon is in a hugely strategic position because it will allow humans to build a base from which they can springboard farther into the solar system—to Mars and beyond.

Why are both public and private entities investing in exploring and using space and the Moon?

Here are some key reasons for the interest. You'll discover more about this in later chapters:

- developing space tourism,
- establishing a base where humans could live long-term,
- learning about our nearest neighbor in space and what its resources could provide us here on Earth,
- using the Moon as a jumping-off point to explore other planets and beyond.

These reasons, naturally, have spurred competition and thus a new space race. This time, the contenders are not just Russia and the United States but also China, which placed a flag on the Moon in 2024, and other countries. In addition, many commercial companies are involved. While the last space race might have been about the challenge of reaching the Moon first, this time the stakes are much higher. Now those in the running want to get to the *best places*—the ones with the valuable resources—on the Moon. It's possible that whoever reaches those spots first—and stays there—will set the standards for those who follow.

The Outer Space Treaty (OST) was written in an era when living for weeks or months on the Moon was an unrealistic fantasy. Now this goal is in sight, and issues could arise that the OST doesn't address. For instance, although Article II clearly states that no country can own the Moon, what about the water and helium there? Can those be owned? If so, who gets to claim them? If countries or companies disagree, how will disputes be resolved? Is there anything like a Space Court?

These are conundrums that are being debated even as you read about them here. You, or your friends, may be among those who will eventually solve such problems. Now is the perfect time to consider how *you* would approach each of these situations and solve the issues of being a citizen of Earth with bases on the Moon and beyond.

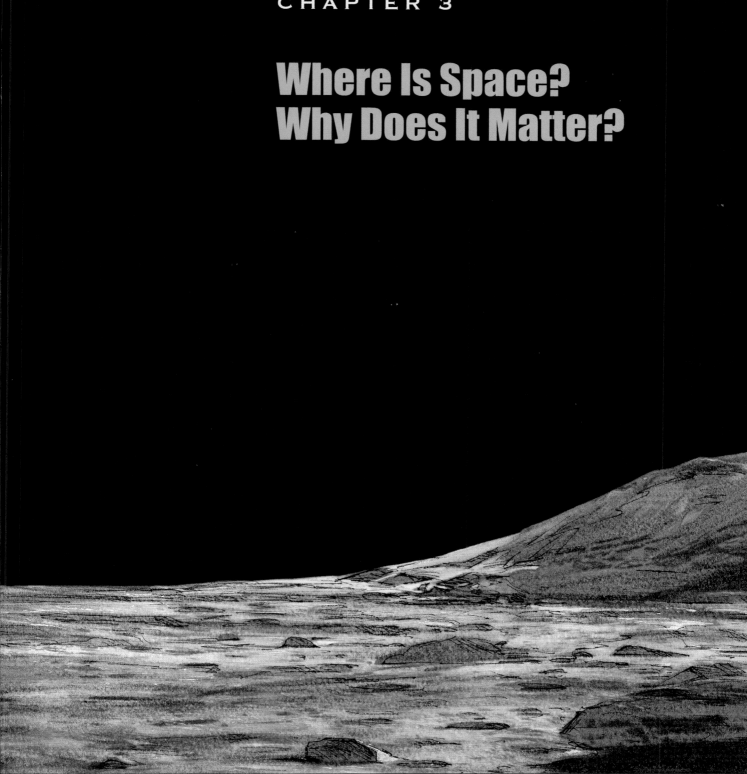

CHAPTER 3

Where Is Space? Why Does It Matter?

Before we say anything more about space—and before you consider heading up there one day—you need to understand a few basic concepts that will help answer the following questions:

- Where does space begin?
- Why does it matter where space begins?

The first question might seem easy. Your answer might be—it's *up there*. After all, if you look up, the stars, the Moon, and a few planets are most likely visible in the night sky. While you are correct, the situation is more complicated than that. Where exactly does space begin? Is it just above the clouds? Is it located at a certain height from the surface of the Earth? Or is it at the point where the stars begin?

The answer depends on whom you ask—a scientist, a politician, a lawyer, or a businessperson. There is no single definition of where space begins that everyone accepts. That creates a conundrum.

What options do we have for defining space? Let's start with the science behind the question.

Layers of Earth's Atmosphere

Earth is surrounded by a mixture of gases that make up its atmosphere. The atmosphere holds much of the heat from the sun, providing us with a relatively stable temperature, and oxygen to breathe. At the same time, the atmosphere screens out harmful ultraviolet rays from the sun. In other words, Earth's atmosphere is what makes life possible on our planet.

Our atmosphere is divided into five layers. The densest layer is closest to Earth.

As you go up from the ground, each layer of the atmosphere becomes thinner and has different characteristics. Note that not all scientists agree on the specific heights of these different layers. The ones listed on the next text page are accepted averages.

Opposite: **The waning gibbous Moon photographed from the ISS as it orbits 262 miles above the Swiss Alps.**

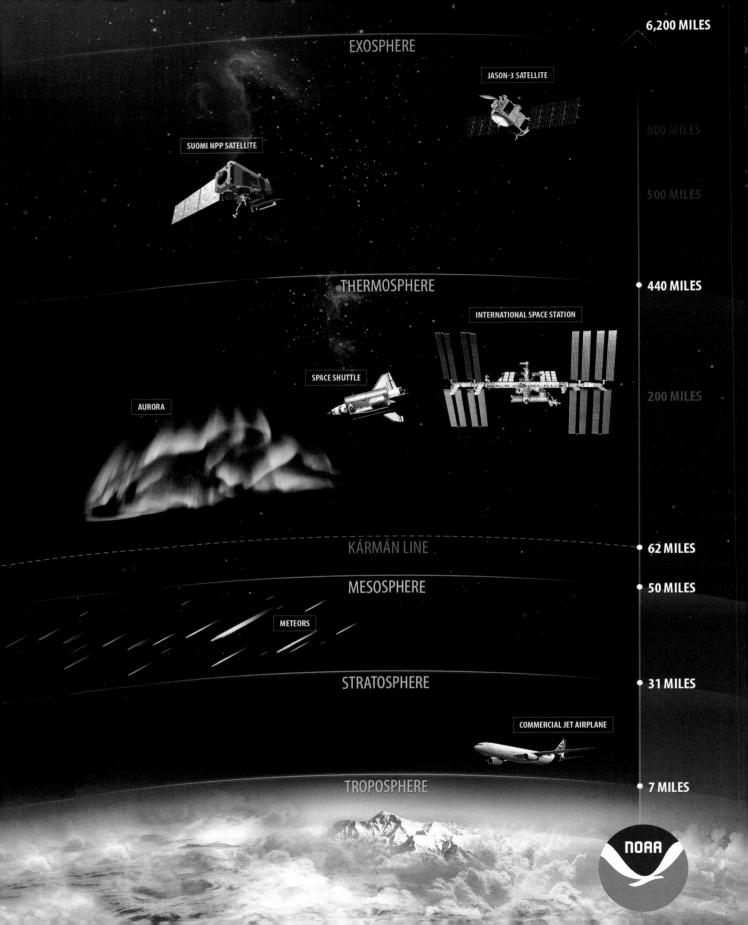

- Troposphere: from the ground up to between 6.2 and 10 miles (10 and 16 km). However, many people assume that the troposphere ends at approximately 7.5 miles (12 km) above the Earth's surface. This is where, for the most part, above-ground life exists and clouds form. Most of our weather happens in this layer.

- Stratosphere: from about 7.5 miles (12 km) to 31 miles (50 km) above the surface. This is where the ozone layer is located. Ultraviolet (UV) rays from the sun are absorbed here and converted to heat for the planet. Commercial planes fly at the lower level of this layer; military aircraft can fly at higher levels.

- Mesosphere: from approximately 31 miles (50 km) to 53 miles (85 km) above the surface. This layer has the coldest temperatures in the Earth's atmosphere, at -130 degrees Fahrenheit (-90 degrees Celsius). Meteors burn up in this layer.

- Thermosphere: from about 53 miles (85 km) to about 375 miles (600 km). Some people believe that the thermosphere stretches even higher, up to 440 miles (700 km). In this layer, the air is extremely thin and the temperatures are cold, but not as cold as the mesosphere because the sun's UV rays are absorbed in this layer. The International Space Station and many satellites are in this layer, and this is also where the Northern and Southern Lights occur.

- Exosphere: from about 440 miles (600 km) to 6,200 miles (10,000 km) above the Earth's surface. Some scientists define it as extending even farther—to 120,000 miles (190,000 km). Air is almost nonexistent in this layer. Most authorities consider this to be outer space, which makes sense, because according to some scientists, the far edge of this layer is halfway to the Moon!

Have you noticed where man-made objects, like commercial planes and satellites, are located? Objects and their location within the layers of the atmosphere help to define where space begins. For example, airplanes don't fly in space, but satellites do orbit in space. That is an important idea to understand.

Now that you've seen the different layers of atmosphere, where do *you* think space begins? Ask your friends, your parents, your teachers. Do they agree? No? That is not surprising. People from different countries and organizations on

Is the ISS in Space?

Is the International Space Station actually in space? The ISS orbits Earth at about 250 miles (400 km) above sea level. That places it solidly in the thermosphere, which is definitely an upper atmosphere of the Earth. Some people believe that space begins at 100 km, where the Kármán line occurs. However, others believe that outer space may not begin until a distance halfway to the Moon. If that's the case, the ISS is not in space. It just depends on whom you ask.

Earth have their own views about space. With all these conflicting ideas, how is it possible to determine where space begins?

To find that answer, it's best to begin at a time when the limits of outer space were first being explored.

Back in the 1950s, the military and many companies in the US were focused on creating airplanes that could fly higher, faster, and farther than ever before. Pi-lots were pushing their planes to the very limits of their mechanical capabilities.

Could an airplane safely fly to the edge of space or beyond? Engineers needed to establish where space begins to figure that out. The first step was determining the height at which airplanes could no longer fly.

Planes need the force of lift to fly. Lift occurs as air flows across the wings from the front to the back of the plane. This air movement counteracts the aircraft's weight and the force of gravity, which allows the plane to fly.

Air in the atmosphere helps to generate lift. As the plane flies to higher altitudes, the air gets thinner. Thinner air is less dense, which means that it can't provide much lift.

To increase the force of lift, airplanes must fly faster in order to stay in the air. But if an airplane does not have a powerful enough engine, it will not be able to

Illustration of the force of lift.

Lift is a mechanical force generated by a solid object moving through a fluid.

Lift

Drag

Thrust

Weight

44

reach the speed needed to push into space. An airplane that cannot achieve orbit must drop back to a lower altitude where the air is denser.

The minimum speed for a craft to reach space and stay there is 17,500 mph. That speed is also required for a craft to remain in orbit around the Earth. Airplanes cannot fly that fast.

Why is it important to identify the point in the atmosphere where the air is too thin for a plane to fly? Until recently, many engineers agreed that this point—where a plane needs to either achieve orbit or drop to a lower altitude—was the edge of space.

Thus NASA, the US military, and the Federal Aviation Administration (FAA)—the agency that controls the airspace over the US—have believed since the 1950s that the edge of space is at 50 miles (80 km) above sea level. In fact, when test pilots first achieved that height, the US Air Force awarded them astronaut pins.

But does everyone agree that 50 miles (80 km) above sea level is the edge of space?

Two states beg to differ with NASA, the US military, and the FAA. Both Virginia and New Mexico have considered passing laws that stipulate where space begins. For Virginia, the location is "at or above 62.5 miles from the Earth's mean sea level." For New Mexico, it's "any location beyond altitudes of 60,000 feet (11.4 miles) above the Earth's mean sea level."

Why are they doing this? These states believe these new definitions of space might help them to attract private spaceflight companies.

Does the rest of the US agree with them? Not really. But the United States is not willing to take a stand on the subject of where space begins. It prefers to see how various technologies evolve before agreeing to a global definition.

So what about other countries? What measures do they use to demarcate the edge of space?

The Kármán Line

In 1957, Hungarian physicist and engineer Theodore von Kármán suggested that the point at which the atmosphere is too thin for airplanes to fly normally is approximately 60 miles (100 km) above sea level. This altitude is designated as the Kármán Line.

While this invisible line may or may not be at exactly 60 miles (100 km), the Kármán Line is accepted by the

The Bogotá Declaration

In 1976, eight countries along the equator issued a statement. They claimed that because satellites in GEO orbit are constantly overhead, and since GEO has limited room, equatorial countries should be able to control the space above their territory.

1. Ecuador
2. Colombia
   (Bogatá is capital)
3. Brazil
4. Congo
5. Democratic Republic
   of the Congo
   (formerly Zaire)
6. Uganda
7. Kenya
8. Indonesia

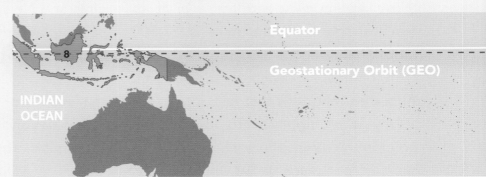

Fédération Aéronautique Internationale, which maintains world records for astronautics and aeronautics. As for countries, only Denmark and Australia officially accept the Kármán Line as the beginning of space. Do most countries agree that space starts below 60 miles (100 km)? Many do, but not all. At least one country sees space starting much, much higher. Colombia has gone so far as to state in its constitution that space begins at geostationary orbit (GEO), which is about 22,237 miles (35,786 km) above Earth's surface.

Because there is so much uncertainty, the United Nations has taken up the issue—but not with much success. The UN Committee on the Peaceful Uses of Outer Space (COPUOS) has been discussing the issue since 1967 and still can't come to an agreement.

Why Does It Matter Where Space Begins?

When you get down—or up—to it, why does it matter where space begins? Who cares whether everyone agrees or not? Here's where the lawyers, government officials, and businesspeople come in.

Every country owns and controls the area above its territory where planes, drones, and balloons generally fly. This is known as sovereign airspace.

Countries negotiate with each other

46

Most other countries believe that this Bogotá Declaration contradicts the Outer Space Treaty, which doesn't allow countries to own space. Nevertheless, two additional countries on the equator have since signed the Bogotá Declaration, hoping to control the number of satellites in GEO.

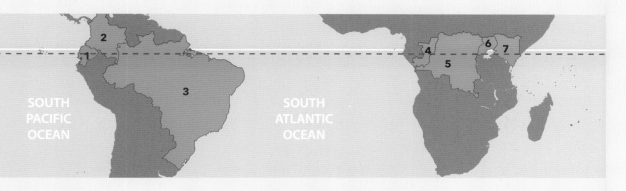

SOUTH PACIFIC OCEAN

SOUTH ATLANTIC OCEAN

about whether aircraft can fly over them (no enemies allowed!), how much noise and pollution they can make, and who's responsible if there's an accident in midair. In the US, the FAA grants—or refuses—permissions and manages the air traffic control system. The National Transportation Safety Board investigates accidents. If unauthorized aircraft enter US airspace, the military is informed and considers taking action.

So, sovereign airspace is not only monitored but also controlled. The situation is different, though, when it comes to the area *above* airspace.

As you saw in Chapter 1 ("Flags on the Moon"), the Outer Space Treaty does not allow countries to own or take control of outer space. This vast region beyond sovereign airspace is "the province of all" humankind and "not subject to appropriation by claim of sovereignty."

Any country or company can launch a satellite or a shuttle and fly it over other countries without their permission once it reaches space. In fact, they do it all the time. Therefore, air law, which requires permission to overfly, and space law, which cannot, contradict each other.

This contradiction would not be a problem if everyone knew and agreed on where airspace ends and outer space begins. But they don't. This is definitely a conundrum. Without a shared understanding, you get the possibility for a lot of discussion, disagreement, lawsuits, and even aggressive action.

Friend or Foe?

On or about January 20, 2023: A Chinese balloon, 200 feet tall, departs Hainan Island, off the southern coast of China. US military and intelligence agencies believe it contains surveillance equipment and begin tracking it. The balloon heads toward Guam, a US territory in the Pacific Ocean.

January 24: The balloon suddenly veers north toward the continental US. Observers do not know whether the change in direction is intentional or caused by a severe cold front shifting the jet stream in which the balloon is riding.

January 28: The balloon enters American airspace over Alaska. Chinese officials do not request or receive permission to enter US airspace. US officials express concern that it carries an apparatus for spying.

January 30: China denies that the balloon has surveillance capabilities and accuses the US of sending ten unauthorized balloons over Chinese airspace in the last year. American officials deny the charge.

January 30–31: The balloon enters Canadian airspace, then floats back into the US over Idaho. US officials consider shooting it down but decide not to because of risk to people on the ground.

February 1: Passengers on a commercial airplane over Billings, Montana, spot the balloon high above them. All air traffic is temporarily halted at the Billings airport. The balloon hovers over a military base in Montana.

February 2: The balloon continues heading southeast.

February 3: In response to the unauthorized presence of the balloon over US territory, Secretary of State Blinken postpones a diplomatic visit to China.

February 4: On orders from President Biden, a US fighter jet shoots down the balloon off the coast of South Carolina and recovers the payload. In response, Chinese officials refuse to return a phone call from US Defense Secretary Lloyd Austin III. The Chinese government calls the Americans' act "a serious violation of international practice" and adds that it "reserves the right to make further responses if necessary."

Opposite: High altitude Chinese balloon photographed over central US airspace by US Air Force on February 3, 2023. *Inset:* Route of balloon across the globe.

The Chinese balloon passed over the United States at a height of 60,000 feet (about 11 miles, or 18 km). There is wide agreement that this put it in US sovereign airspace. And because the Chinese did not receive permission to send a balloon into that area, the US military stated that it had the right to shoot the balloon down.

That height, however, is at the lower edge of a region that the military and politicians in several countries call "near space." It stretches from 60,000 to 330,000 feet or about 11 to 62 miles (17 to 100 km) above Earth. This is an area where neither air law nor space law clearly applies—an area that could possibly be entered without permission and, therefore, without consequences. Who's in charge of near space? Who knows? It is literally "undefined."

New technologies are also raising questions about the transition from airspace to outer space—questions with legal and possibly military consequences. Most spacecraft are launched vertically, or straight up. In the past, however, some vehicles—such as the space shuttle— were launched and landed more like typical airplanes. Thus, they were on a trajectory that could possibly cross the airspace of other countries.

In the future, will there be more spacecraft launched like airplanes? It's possible. If that happens, would this spacecraft be allowed to fly over a nearby foreign country? The spacecraft could claim what is called "a right of innocent passage"—that it was just passing through on its way to outer space. But some countries might object, saying that an unwanted spacecraft was violating their airspace.

Various businesses would also like to clarify where airspace ends and outer space begins. For example, some space tourism companies and insurance companies (and space lawyers) want to know which laws, if any, apply to them.

By now the answer to the question "Where does space begin?" should be about as clear as mud. There is no single global definition. But if you accept that space begins somewhere between 50 and 60 miles (80 and 100 km) above the Earth, you're probably good.

Now let's take a look at space itself. Like Earth's atmosphere, it's described as a series of layers.

Layers of Space

Just as in the atmosphere, space is defined by different layers. In this case they are called orbits, since they are defined based on their location relative to the Earth.

"Orbit" can be a verb, as when an object "orbits" the Earth. It can also be a noun, meaning the area above the planet where a satellite is located. Each orbit described below has different characteristics.

If you compare the orbits of space and the layers of Earth's atmosphere, you'll notice that they overlap.

- low Earth orbit (LEO)—begins from 100 to 180 miles (62 to 290 km) and extends up to 1,243 miles (2,000 km) above the Earth's surface. (Again, not everyone agrees on this starting point.)
- medium Earth orbit (MEO)—from 1,243 to 22,237 miles (2,000 to 35,786 km).

- geostationary Earth orbit (GEO)— 22,237 miles (35,786 km). This falls exactly over the equator.
- geosynchronous orbit (GSO)— occurs at the same height as GEO, but in this case, the object is positioned so that it is in sync with Earth's orbit.
- high Earth orbit (HEO)—higher than 22,237 miles (35,786 km).
- cislunar space—from high Earth orbit (HEO) to the Moon's orbit.

This bulleted list and the illustration below describe where these layers are located. The limits for each of these areas are approximate—there isn't a universally agreed-upon range for each layer.

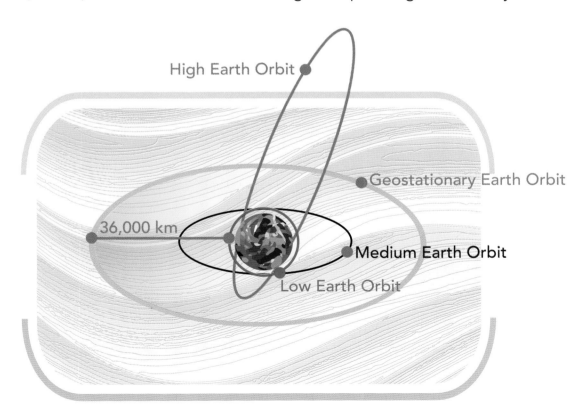

High Earth Orbit

Geostationary Earth Orbit

36,000 km

Medium Earth Orbit

Low Earth Orbit

Where is space located? Layers of Earth's atmosphere. Layers in space. Cislunar space. Whew. That's a lot of concepts to understand. And it's why we put this information here in one chapter, where it's easy to access. Feel free to come back to this chapter and review it as you read more of the book.

Next up? We'll explore how countries (and companies) on Earth live and work together in space.

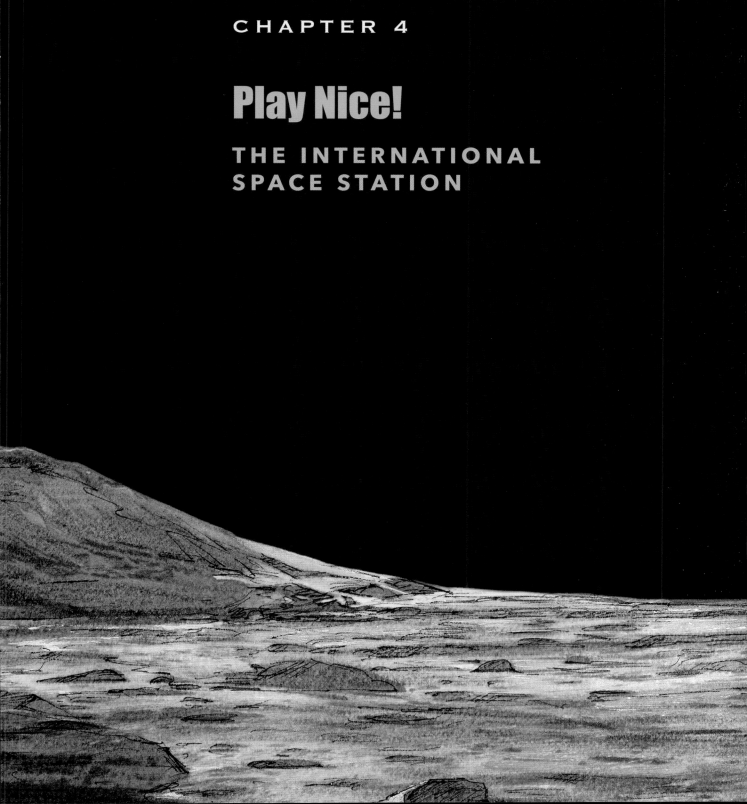

CHAPTER 4

Play Nice!

THE INTERNATIONAL SPACE STATION

Expedition 1: Where's the Light Switch?

"Six meters. Five. Four."

Mission commander William "Bill" Shepherd counted down the narrowing gap between the Soyuz rocket and the International Space Station while cosmonaut Yuri Gidzenko handled the delicate maneuvers. Two days earlier, on a foggy October 31, 2000, Shepherd, Gidzenko, and his fellow Russian Sergei Krikalev had blasted off in the Soyuz from the Baikonur Cosmodrome in Kazakhstan. After four years of training together at various sites in Russia and the Johnson Space Center in Houston, Texas, the trio were finally approaching the ISS—their home in low Earth orbit for the next four and a half months.

That timeline assumed they could make the station safe for human habitation. For the last two years, astronauts from five space agencies—in the US, Russia, Canada, Japan, and Europe—had worked together to build the ISS piece by piece in space. Theoretically the ISS was ready for occupancy, but so far no one had ever spent so much as a night there, let alone cooked dinner or gone to the bathroom. Shepherd, Gidzenko, and Krikalev would be the first to do so. They were Expedition 1.

"Three. Two. One."

"We've arrived!" Krikalev announced.

Left to right: Yuri Gidzenko, Soyuz commander; astronaut William "Bill" Shepherd, mission commander; and cosmonaut Sergei Krikalev, flight engineer.

The team pumped fists to share their excitement, and then got busy. After equalizing the pressure between the rocket and the station, Shepherd pointed to the hatch and turned to Krikalev, indicating "After you." Although the American was the commander, the Russians had more experience in space, and Shepherd wanted one of them to have the honor of entering the ISS first.

Krikalev floated into the dark module and exclaimed, "Somebody has to turn on the lights." He felt for the switch and flipped it down. The lights worked. But would anything else? They needed to figure that out ASAP.

In ninety minutes, the ISS's orbit would take them over Europe, where they were to conduct a live audio-video feed from space. Muttering in a mixture of Russian and English that the teammates called Runglish, they hunted for the television cable, hooked it up, and checked the radio frequency for sound.

"It was frantic," Shepherd later said. "We were scrambling."

The radio crackled and they heard, "We're in contact!" Engineers on the ground near Moscow and in Houston applauded as they watched the American and the two Russians clasp gloved hands.

Their live appearance complete, the crew turned to their long to-do list. Next up: Figure out how to turn on the hot water. Connect the toilet. Crank up the oxygen. Scrub the air of excess carbon dioxide. Turn on—but, first, they discovered, rebuild—the computer system. In short, make the place livable.

Meanwhile, the ISS continued to circle the Earth every ninety minutes, coming into contact with ground control in Houston and then, twenty-five minutes later, in Moscow. In addition to the schedule that the crew was to follow, each group of Earth-based engineers had its own ideas about how the guys in space should spend their time. So once the basic checks were complete, engineers on the ground felt the need to give instructions. The result was that the ISS crew received one set of directions as they flew over Texas and another when they passed over Moscow. It was confusing and frustrating, to say the least. After several weeks of conflicting instructions, Shepherd got fed up.

"We are the *International* Space Station," he reminded them. "You two guys gotta get your act together, then call us. We're going to execute one plan, not one for Moscow and one for Houston."

And they did. Shepherd rejoiced. "That was the happiest day in space!"

The multinational team 250 miles overhead had to teach the earthlings how to cooperate.

Getting Along in Space

This debut voyage of the ISS set the stage for at least a quarter century of cooperation among rotating members of international teams. More than 250 astronauts, from at least nineteen countries, have lived and worked on the ISS, the largest and most complex structure ever put into space.

But the ISS didn't come out of nowhere. Steps toward creating partnerships among multiple countries had begun long before Expedition 1. From the very beginning, the law that established the National Aeronautics and Space Administration (NASA) in 1958 required it to cooperate "with other nations and groups of nations" for the benefit of humankind. Over the years, NASA has worked hard with more than 120 countries to carry out this mission in thousands of ways.

Building the International Space Station–in Space!

How did the ISS come together? Teamwork.

Before the actual building of the ISS could begin, the complex legal and political guidelines for working together had to be outlined. In 1998, sixteen countries signed agreements establishing multinational partnerships to construct the ISS.

These arrangements named NASA as the lead agency and clarified that each country would provide whatever equipment it needed—ranging from waste water devices to treadmills—and control its own module on the ISS. That meant that basically each module functioned like the country's own sovereign land— each country had the final say over what happened in its module.

Once the legal agreements were in place, the US, Canada, Europe, Japan, and Russia began the massive job of designing and building the ISS. The first control module, called *Zarya* (or "sunrise"), was to be assembled by the Russians. The US had the job of building the *Unity* module and a small tunnel which would connect the two structures.

The construction of America's piece of the ISS was put on display for all to see. Anyone who traveled to the Kennedy Space Center in the early 1990s could peek through the windows of the NASA clean room and see *Unity* being built.

Work on the ISS was progressing in the US, Canada, and Russia as each country built its separate parts. Then

A Monumental Meeting in Space

Zarya was launched atop a Russian Proton rocket on November 20, 1998, and established its position in low Earth orbit. The US space shuttle *Endeavour* was launched a few weeks later, on December 4, with the STS-88 mission shuttle crew. It took two days to catch up with the *Zarya* module in space. Using the Canadarm (a remote-controlled robotic arm on the space shuttle), the crew grabbed *Zarya* and attached it to the ISS. With exact precision, the astronauts maneuvered *Zarya* into position above the *Unity* module until . . . click . . . the two were connected. It was a historic achievement! While neither of these modules had ever met on Earth, they were now joined in space.

 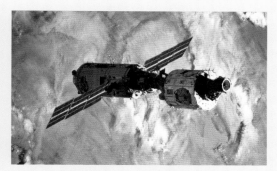

Left, *Zarya* being positioned to join with *Unity*; *bottom*, full view of the ISS, March 2011.

Construction proceeded over the next ten years, with regular visits by various US space shuttle crews and Russian's Proton Rocket, which was unmanned. Eventually the manned Russian Soyuz rocket was also launched. All brought more pieces of the ISS into space. As the countries continued to cooperate, the ISS kept expanding, with more modules, more laboratories and living spaces, and even a cupola (observatory) for everyone to enjoy the amazing views of space and Earth. In all, forty-two different launches were used to construct the ISS—thirty-seven on US space shuttles and five on Russian rocket.

NASA engineers worked with Russian, Canadian, and European engineers at Kennedy Space Center to design and build the ISS. But when they began working together, it was clear that the three countries needed new ways to communicate. It was challenging at times because the US was the only country that was not on the metric system. But even more significant was that each country had its own way of doing things.

For example, when the Russians provided their *Zvezda* module for the ISS, the NASA engineers noticed one thing right away: all the equipment on board was loud—too loud for OSHA (Occupational Safety and Health Administration) requirements. This meant that it was against US government guidelines for astronauts to be in that area for longer than eight hours a day, because it could damage their hearing.

The Russians, however, had no such restrictions from their government. In fact, they had been using this type of module on the Mir space station for quite a while. Many discussions ensued to figure out how to fix the problem.

Of course the US engineers had to be diplomatic in their approach, and they had to come up with suggestions that were agreeable to the Russians for how to muffle the noisy machines. This "tiny" problem took a couple of months to fix, as the American and Russian engineers bridged not only engineering design issues but also language challenges. And yet they successfully fixed the problem. This was a testament to how well the two countries worked together in space.

Training the Crew to Live and Work Together

The successful development of an international space station requires precise engineering that ensures all parts fit together. It also requires training crews to work together seamlessly. After all, crew members must rely on each other daily for survival.

No one can go to the ISS unless they sign the Code of Conduct for the International Space Station Crew. This essential document establishes a chain of command and sets out safety and health procedures, as well as other requirements to "maintain a harmonious and cohesive relationship." For example, "[the crew] shall comply with the ISS Commander's orders, all Flight and ISS program Rules, operational directives, and management policies." And that's just for starters.

The very first ISS team had a lot to learn. By the time cosmonaut Sergei

Krikalev joined the team, he had already spent a couple of years training and then living with French and British astronauts on Russia's Mir space station. He was used to handling different languages and customs. Although Bill Shepherd had worked with military counterparts in other countries, he had less international experience than Krikalev.

When Shepherd arrived at the training facility in Star City, northeast of Moscow, he assumed that the Russian and US (NASA) training would be similar and conducted in English. He got a surprise. Russian cosmonauts trained very differently from American astronauts. The Russians, he discovered, relied much less on computer simulations, diagrams, and documentation than the Americans. Shepherd realized, "The only way I was going to understand how these guys thought was if I could talk to them." So he worked hard to become fluent in Russian. He also learned local customs. For instance, he and his crewmates were blessed by a Russian Orthodox priest before launch. And, for good luck, they followed a tradition begun by Yuri Gagarin and peed on a tire of the bus ferrying them to the launch site.

Shepherd and NASA engineers learned so much from their partners—sharing equipment, technical know-how, problem-solving, and communications techniques—that Shepherd concluded, "Without the Russians, we would not have a space station."

Who's in Charge on the ISS?

Being selected as the commander of the ISS is a huge honor. The commander is responsible for maintaining a safe, pleasant, respectful environment for all crew members on board. The commander must also ensure that the day-to-day operations on the ISS follow the missions set forth by the flight director. That may include giving assignments to the team and ensuring that missions are completed.

The mission commander is chosen by an agreement among the countries participating in the ISS. For the first fifteen missions, the US and Russia alternated the position of ISS commander. In 2009, on Expedition 21, the first commander from the European Space Agency was chosen for the ISS. Since then, the position of commander has not followed a strict pattern but is mutually agreed upon among the countries.

BENEFITS OF THE ISS

Life on the ISS has changed a lot since the very first mission. there may be six to thirteen crew members on the ISS at any given time. The teams consist of astronauts from the US, Russia, Japan, Canada, the European Space Agency, and several other countries, including the United Arab Emirates (UAE). In March 2023, UAE's first astronaut, Sultan Al Neyadi, joined the ISS crew.

One of the main reasons for building the ISS was to learn how humans can live and work in a microgravity environment. Thousands of hours of exciting research have been conducted on the ISS.

The space agencies have learned how microgravity acts on the human body, and how to eat, sleep, and go to the bathroom in space. They know that plants grown in space produce fruits and vegetables that are just as tasty as those grown on Earth.

In the last 24 years, over 3,300 experiments have been conducted aboard the station. Its unique microgravity environment offers opportunities to investigate many scientific topics in ways not available on Earth. What have we learned?

Bottom: NASA's "Veggie" plant growth system on the ISS allows astronauts to grow and eat fresh fruits and vegetables. One day, this same system may be used at a base on the Moon.

Right: Crew members on Expedition 60 take turns capturing images of the rapidly intensifying Hurricane Dorian from the cupola inside the International Space Station on Aug. 30, 2019, as it churned over the Atlantic Ocean.

The list is long and keeps growing, but here are a few of the highlights:

- **Sequencing DNA in space.** This breakthrough enables us to diagnose diseases and keep astronauts healthy. It also holds the potential to identify DNA in other parts of the universe, opening up a new realm of exploration.
- **Producing artificial retinas.** When perfected, this technology can potentially restore vision to people on Earth who have lost it due to disease or injury.
- **Creating a new X-ray technology** that decreases the amount of radiation exposure and allows for better image quality.
- **Growing tumors in space.** Microgravity offers scientists a way to develop and test new chemotherapy drugs to attack cancers creatively.
- **Developing new air filter technology** that could be used on Earth to more effectively purify air and remove contaminants, including infectious airborne viruses.
- **Providing opportunities for students** to engage in science without the confines of Earth's gravity. NASA sends many student-led experiments to space for testing. This open support of education inspires many young learners to seek out careers in STEM.

Astronauts have learned how to maintain a habitat in space. That isn't an easy task, given that the nearest hardware store or equipment depot is more than 250 miles away—and getting there requires a special spacecraft.

They have recorded thousands of hours of video of our planet—enough to analyze and learn about weather patterns, watch hurricanes form and volcanoes erupt, and even watch water levels rise and fall.

Astronauts on the ISS have launched hundreds of satellites into orbit around our planet. Some of them were designed to provide information about the Earth, while others aided communications on Earth or were sent into deep space to conduct research. Many of these satellites were created by other countries, and some were made by students!

The ISS has offered an excellent way to gather information about humans living in microgravity. Now NASA and its partners plan to take that information and use it to establish a long-term presence on the Moon.

But life in microgravity is not immune to politics and actions back on Earth. Sometimes issues arise. You'll learn more about that in Chapter 5 ("Spats and Mishaps").

Left: Nicole Mann and Frank Rubio inside the seven-window cupola on the ISS; *right:* Catherine (Cady) Coleman washes her hair aboard ISS.

A Day on the ISS

What do astronauts do during the day on the ISS?

They wake up and start their day around 6 a.m. Greenwich Mean Time (GMT)—the time zone observed on the ISS. Some take showers, if they didn't do so before going to bed. Others might head to the kitchen to start making breakfast after getting dressed. Then they brush their teeth and get to work!

First up on the job front? Checking their schedule for the day. While they were sleeping, Mission Control, which alternates between NASA and Russia's space agency, Roscosmos, was awake (and

working). It has mapped out what tasks each astronaut must complete that day.

After a quick lunch, one or two of the crew might head to the treadmill or bicycle for their workouts. Every astronaut must work out at least two and a half hours a day, doing physical exercises that include weight or resistance training.

The afternoon is spent doing more tasks or working out, depending on what the astronaut did in the morning.

Around 7:30 p.m., crew members do their end-of-day check-in with Mission Control. After everything is set, they head off for dinner. For the next

Top, Jessica Watkins and Bob Hines study farming in space;
right, Koichi Wakata strapped into his sleeping bag in his sleep station;
bottom right, Josh Cassada cleaning hardware.

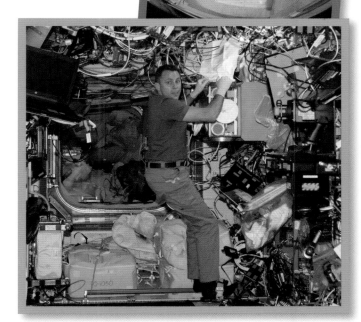

two hours they can eat dinner, watch a movie, stare out of the cupola at the amazing sights, or talk to their families. Bedtime is around 9:30 p.m., because the next busy day is only a short eight hours away.

Not everyone on the ISS is an astronaut. Civilians have joined the crew for short periods of time, which we'll discuss in Chapter 9 ("Selfies in Space"). But regardless of who is on board, they are all there to work together, to perform scientific research, and to learn about living and working in microgravity.

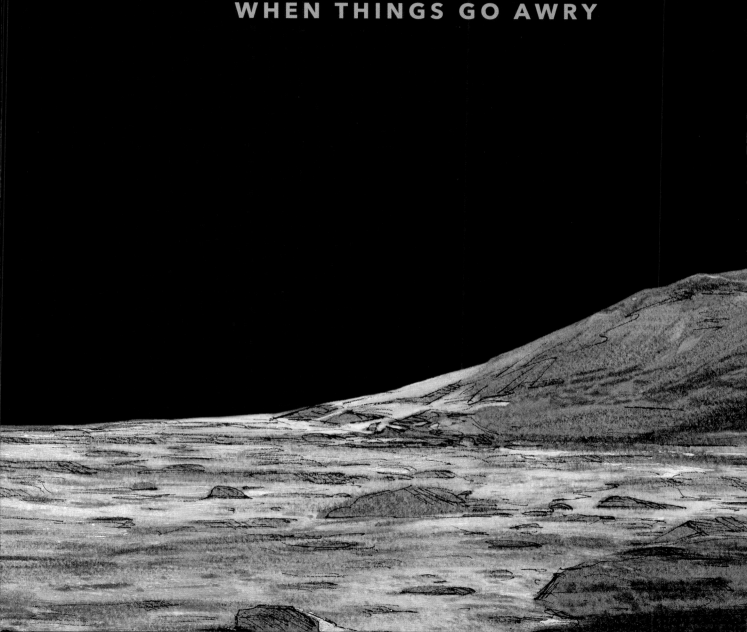

Spats and Mishaps

WHERE TO TURN
WHEN THINGS GO AWRY

Mars, Here We Come! Oops, No We Don't

Russian and European scientists and engineers were tremendously excited in early 2022. They had been working together for thirteen years on the ExoMars program, building the Rosalind Franklin rover. Its scheduled launch was just a few months away. If everything went according to plan, it would land on Mars and begin looking for life—either present or in the past—on that volcanic red planet.

The engineers had designed the rover so that it could roll over rocky terrain, finding the best path without guidance from humans on Earth, and then drill down 2 meters (6½ feet) into Martian soil. That depth is necessary to avoid the cosmic rays that might have destroyed evidence of life. Then the rover would scoop material into its onboard laboratory and analyze the contents. Finally, the Rosalind Franklin would relay the results to curious scientists on Earth. Maybe soon the world would learn whether anything had ever lived—or was still living—in the dried lakes on Mars!

But on February 24, 2022, things stopped going according to plan. Russia invaded its neighbor Ukraine. And on March 17, cooperation between Roscosmos and the European Space Agency (ESA) abruptly ended. A representative from the ESA announced, "We deeply deplore the human casualties and tragic consequences of aggression towards Ukraine. While recognizing the impact on scientific exploration of space, ESA is fully aligned with the sanctions imposed on Russia."

The twenty-two European countries that make up the ESA agreed that they could no longer work with the Russians on anything related to space, even if it meant canceling a trip to Mars. Dmitry Rogozin, director general of Roscosmos, quickly showed his displeasure. He posted on a social media platform, "If you block cooperation with us, who will save the ISS from uncontrolled deorbiting and falling into the United States?"

Was he threatening the International Space Station? That's the place where everyone, no matter where they're from, has gotten along for more than two decades. Actually, he *was* doing just that. Even worse, he was implying that Russia would abandon the astronauts on board the ISS and allow it to drop out of space and crash-land someplace in America.

Scientists' moods swiftly spun from elation to deep concern.

When Problems Arise

Whether or not countries are able to work well with each other depends on many factors—their languages, customs, history, geography, natural resources, leaders, religions, and values. Often governments may be at odds on the ground while their citizens remain friendly in space.

This has happened periodically since the beginning of the Cold War. In 1999, for instance, US President Bill Clinton ranted at Russian Premier Boris Yeltsin for laying siege to the neighboring Republic of Chechnya. Nevertheless, the ISS's Expedition 1 crew of Bill Shepherd, Yuri Gidzenko, and Sergei Krikalev kept training together. Typically, scientific research in space has not been affected when politics become heated on Earth.

But the political and scientific fallout from Russian aggression in 2022 was different. The European Space Agency stopped cooperating with Russia on its Mars program and also on three joint Moon missions. In response, Rogozin threatened to prevent the ISS's rocket thrusters from firing, which he implied would affect the orbiting capability of the ISS. If the thrusters were not fired, it was possible that the ISS would not be able to maintain enough speed to stay in orbit, and it might enter Earth's atmosphere and eventually crash into the ocean.

Would that be possible? Does Russia control the rocket thrusters on the ISS?

Russian unmanned vehicle Progress docked to *Zvezda*. Note thrusters on *Zvezda*.

Zvezda Module—Rocket Power for the ISS

The *Zvezda* module, which was connected to the ISS in 2000, was created solely by the Russians and contains some important equipment. It is the living quarters for the cosmonauts on the ISS. But more importantly, it is also the one module equipped with thrusters—sixteen small thrusters and two larger ones—for keeping the ISS in proper orbit.

Why must the thrusters be fired regularly? The ISS is in a reasonably stable orbit. But like every other object in space, it is in constant free fall. Free fall is the term used to describe an object affected by no other force than gravity. In this case, objects in space are affected by Earth's gravity. The force of Earth's gravity is so strong that it can pull objects toward it, even when they are thousands of miles away in space. This force is not as strong in space as the gravitational force felt on Earth, but it still exists.

So as the ISS orbits the planet, it is gradually pulled back toward Earth. Firing the thrusters creates a forward motion, which is stronger than the force of gravity, so the ISS stays at the desired orbital height. This operation is called station-keeping.

Yes. The ISS's thrusters are on the Russian module. Since each country owns and operates its modules, Russia could refuse to use the thrusters to adjust the ISS's orbit. Is this a big deal? Yes. However, other ways exist to keep the ISS in its proper orbit. Supply spacecraft that visit the station are also capable of doing this. In fact, they regularly perform this operation.

The Russian Progress spacecraft routinely provides the ISS with fuel, food, and other supplies. It blasts off from Baikonur Cosmodrome in Kazakhstan on a Soyuz rocket, it docks with the ISS, and the astronauts remove the supplies. While the *Progress* is connected to the ISS, it can fire its rocket boosters to keep the ISS in the proper orbit. The concern? The Russians own the Progress.

Is it possible that Rogozin's threat to bring his boosters and cosmonauts home might have been real? Not exactly. Northrop Grumman, a US corporation, has been successfully resupplying the ISS since 2013 with its Cygnus spacecraft. In 2018, a test determined that Cygnus could also provide boosting capabilities to the ISS. And in February 2022—the very same month Russia invaded Ukraine—Cygnus headed up to the ISS for another resupply. A very timely coincidence, as Cygnus was likely already scheduled for this trip. It was good to have Cygnus there, just in case . . .

Cygnus capture with Canadarm2.

The Outer Space Treaty and the Rescue Agreement: Go Get That Astronaut!

Shortly after Rogozin blustered about taking his spaceship and going home, he was removed from his job as the head of Roscosmos. Yuri Borosov, his replacement, quickly made it clear that Russia would continue to participate as a full partner in the International Space Station, at least until sometime after 2024, which was soon extended to 2028.

"The ISS project has enriched world science," he said, "and has united us to some extent. I believe that both today and in the future, such projects should be out of politics."

That was a huge relief. But what if Rogozin had carried out his threat? And what if the cosmonauts on the ISS had agreed to leave and take the Soyuz spacecraft with them? This drastic step might have left the astronauts stranded in space—at least until a Crew Dragon spacecraft could get to them. Since no one has ever taken this action, and everyone hopes no one ever will, this scenario presents hypothetical "what-ifs." But would abandoning astronauts be legal if someone did it?

The Outer Space Treaty has some answers to this question because it lays out principles on how countries should treat each other and their astronauts. Let's look at the OST. ("States" in the treaty means countries.)

Article V
States . . . shall regard astronauts as envoys of mankind in outer space and shall render to them all possible assistance in the event of accident, distress, or emergency landing.

Article V refers to astronauts as "envoys" of humankind. This is a poetic turn of phrase that probably sounded noble and futuristic in 1967 when the OST was adopted. After all, very few astronauts were scheduled to orbit Earth or land on a celestial body anytime soon.

Nevertheless, the United Nations con-

sidered Article V so urgent that within two months, the UN also adopted an Agreement on the Rescue of Astronauts and the Return of Objects Launched into Outer Space. This agreement tells countries that they have to conduct search-and-rescue operations for astronauts in distress and their vehicles. It doesn't matter whether they're cosmonauts or Chinese taikonauts, or whether they've dropped into a remote desert or ocean on Earth or gotten stuck on the far side of the Moon. It doesn't matter how they ended up there. Someone must retrieve them and get them home.

The moral—and the law—is that spacefarers cannot be left behind.

The Outer Space Treaty: It's Worldwide

You might remember from the Introduction that treaties have the force of law. So the Outer Space Treaty is a legal document. Not only that, but the OST includes all international laws—every single one. Here's what those are and how the OST addresses them.

Article III
States . . . shall carry on activities in the exploration and use of outer space . . . in accordance with international law.

There are laws in the state and country where you live against crimes like murder and stealing. These laws exist because legislatures, or other law-making bodies—like Congress in the United States or the Bundestag in Germany—have adopted them.

There is no legislature for the world. Nevertheless, there are international laws that countries must follow. How can that be?

International law comes from two main sources:

- *Written* documents, including treaties, agreements, and declarations that government officials sign, often with great ceremony. Examples include treaties that protect the environment or the rights of children.
- *Unwritten* actions, which countries have followed for so many years that the behavior has become ordinary. An example is that enslavement is considered an international crime, even though there's no treaty that says so.

Article III of the OST, in effect, highlights every word of every international law—whether written down or not—and drops them into the OST. So all international laws that nations must abide by on Earth apply to actions in space as well.

This is important because international laws set the rules for all humankind. Whether people are on Earth, in space, or on a celestial body, their rights must be observed. These rights aren't just international anymore—they're universal.

The Outer Space Treaty: The Golden Rule of Space

Article IX
States . . . shall conduct all their activities in outer space . . . with due regard to the corresponding interests of all other States.

Article IX says that countries must think about how their actions in space might affect other countries, and then act accordingly. They shouldn't do anything that will harm either another country or its "envoys in space" (a.k.a. its astronauts). Countries should act the way they would like to be treated. In that way, Article IX can be considered the Golden Rule of the OST.

There is a wrinkle here, however. Article IX says that countries should operate *"with due regard* to the corresponding interests of all other States." What does "due regard" mean specifically? No one knows exactly. In fact, space lawyers debate that a lot.

Other conundrums are also causing people to scratch their heads. For instance:

- Will all emerging spacefaring nations sign on to the OST?
- Will every country that has signed the OST stay on board? Countries can withdraw with one year's notice. No one has done this. But imagine drivers declaring that they plan to start ignoring traffic laws, like stopping for red lights!

The principles embedded in the Outer Space Treaty convey goals and values of how countries should behave and treat each other in space. The OST didn't intend to specify detailed rules of the road, partly because the road to space was just getting built when the OST was written. Recently, additional steps have been taken to start filling in some holes in this remarkable but aging document.

Etiquette Guide to Space: Norms of Behavior

It's far better to avoid spats altogether than to have to figure out how to resolve them once they heat up. The United Nations, many countries, and even businesses are trying to come up with guidelines of good conduct to head off disagreements in space. These guidelines are sometimes called "norms of responsible behavior."

Norms are actions or behaviors that are generally accepted. For instance, if certain groups of kids—say, the soccer team—always sit together at lunch, that's a norm. Norms are different in different cultures. They can be created, changed, and spread around. They can be helpful or hurtful.

Norms for space could include guidelines for how to help astronauts in distress—and, even more importantly, how to keep space travelers from ending up in distress. Norms aren't laws. But remember that eventually, once certain behaviors are accepted by a lot of people over a long period of time, they become international law. Even if they're not written down. After a while, they're not just guidelines: they're legal requirements that everyone must follow. So we want to get the norms right from the very beginning.

The Artemis Accords: An Introduction

When the US decided to return to the Moon and stay there, officials knew they needed to fill in some gaps in the Outer Space Treaty. So, in 2020, NASA and seven other space agencies proposed an additional path to encourage cooperation in space—the Artemis Accords. These are ten statements on how countries should behave in space. We discuss them in Chapter 12 ("Who's In Charge Around Here?").

By May 15, 2024, forty countries had signed the Accords. Russia and China had not. Roscosmos Director Rogozin accused the US of carrying out an "invasion" of the Moon.

The Accords are not legally binding at this point. Still, a growing number of countries share the belief that they can get along with each other on the Moon. One reason is that some space lawyers have put together manuals—called Woomera and MILAMOS—listing every law and rule that countries have agreed to for behaving well in space. There are a lot!

1. Australia
2. Canada
3. Italy
4. Japan
5. Luxembourg
6. United Arab Emirates
7. United States
8. United Kingdom
9. Ukraine
10. South Korea
11. New Zealand
12. Brazil
13. Poland
14. Mexico
15. Israel
16. Romania
17. Bahrain
18. Singapore
19. Colombia
20. France
21. Saudi Arabia
22. Nigeria
23. Rwanda
24. Czech Republic
25. Spain
26. Ecuador
27. India
28. Argentina
29. Germany
30. Iceland
31. Netherlands
32. Bulgaria
33. Angola
34. Belgium
35. Greece
36. Uruguay
37. Switzerland
38. Sweden
39. Slovenia
40. Lithuania

Countries that have signed the Artemis Accords as of May 15, 2024, listed in order of signing.

How Is the Antarctic Like the Moon?

In the 1950s, seven nations were claiming ownership of parts of Antarctica. Some of their claims overlapped, and most of the countries, like France, Norway, and the United Kingdom, weren't anywhere close to the bottom of the globe. Fearing that this remote, frozen area could become a hiding place for nuclear weapons (remember, this was during the Cold War), the US called together a dozen countries. By the end of the decade, they agreed on the Antarctic Treaty, stating that Antarctica should "be used exclusively for peaceful purposes . . . with the interests of science and the progress of all mankind."

Sound familiar? This document was being written at the same time as the Outer Space Treaty. Because it bans military activity, including weapons tests, nuclear explosions, and disposing of radioactive waste, many people look to it as a model for an antiwar agreement in space.

How Are the High Seas Like the Moon?

Like space, the high seas belong to no one but are accessible to anyone (anyone with a ship, that is). That can be a problem, because a country or a company might be able to catch so many tuna fish that there wouldn't be enough left for others. Or they might dump waste in the ocean, killing marine life. There could even be pirates on the high seas beyond national borders.

Fortunately, countries have been working together to address these problems.

- The United Nations Convention on the Law of the Sea created a set of rules for the world to help prevent clashes over borders, taking underwater resources, and piracy. (Just to be clear, no one is predicting space pirates.) Even countries that haven't ratified the Convention on the Law of the Sea follow it.
- The High Seas Treaty, signed by 190 countries in 2023, will protect marine life from overfishing in international waters.

Both efforts show that countries can agree to get along in open spaces—maybe including outer space.

74

China—A Special Case?

To explore the vast cosmos, develop the space industry and build China into a space power is our eternal dream.

—President Xi Jinping, January 2022

China is a major spacefaring nation. But we haven't said much about it, partly because it doesn't participate in the International Space Station. Also, China hasn't signed the Artemis Accords. Why not? And what does this mean for multinational cooperation in space?

The Chinese National Space Administration (CNSA) was formed in 1993, approximately a year after the Chinese began their human spaceflight program. The first spacecraft China developed was based on the Russian Soyuz module, with some minor engineering upgrades. It was called Shenzhou.

It took the CNSA ten years to launch its first taikonaut into space. On October 15, 2003, Yang Liwei became the first human to be launched into space on a Chinese spacecraft. On that day, China became only the third nation on the planet to independently put a human in space—the other two, of course, were the US and Russia.

Some people would say that the three nations that have accomplished so much should work together to further human exploration in space. Certainly, the Outer Space Treaty would make that point. But politics on the ground don't always allow for cooperation in space.

China has agreements with more than three dozen countries—including Russia, Brazil, France, the United Kingdom, and Germany—to continue its impressive achievements in space. But the US and China rarely speak to each other when it comes to matters of space.

The reason dates back to 2011, when US Congressman Frank Wolf got upset with China for stealing American trade secrets. He was also concerned about China's history of human rights abuses, such as forbidding people to practice their religion. In reaction, he convinced Congress to pass a law, the Wolf Amendment, that bans NASA from cooperating with China unless NASA gets an explicit authorization from the FBI and Congress. This requirement makes it almost impossible for the US to collaborate with China on space matters, limiting everyone's knowledge.

For example, American and Chinese

scientists really wanted to talk with each other while they were analyzing data from the Chang'e 1 and Chang'e 2 lunar orbiters. Was that really a hot spot on the far side of the Moon? The Americans couldn't tell for sure, and because their research was funded by NASA, they couldn't call up the engineers in China to ask.

Fortunately, China made some of its databases available to the public. Also, a Chinese planetary scientist there, Jianqing Feng, quit his job and moved to the United States. His reason: "I realized that combining the lunar exploration data from different countries would . . . make exciting findings." Working together, Feng and US scientists concluded that the spot on the Moon had probably once been a rare, Earth-like volcano. This

Photo of a rare, Earth-like volcano on the Moon. Researchers determined that this volcano, called Compton-Belkovich, was once fed by a much larger granite magma chamber below it.

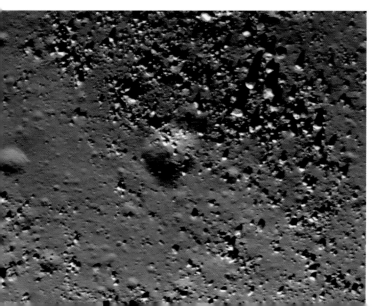

discovery might never have happened if Feng hadn't come to the US and brought his research.

This situation, in which NASA, including NASA-funded scientists, cannot communicate with the CNSA, is an ongoing issue. A big one. It's also one that does not seem to be going away anytime soon. That's because Congress has re-adopted the Wolf Amendment every year when NASA's funding comes up for a vote. As a result, each country has headed off on its own, without sharing technologies or much information.

On Their Own, Doing Fine

China has had impressive results without US help. After the initial accomplishment in 2003, taikonauts performed their first spacewalk in 2008. And in September 2011, the CNSA launched Tiangong 1, its first space lab. It was to be used for research and practice in docking a spacecraft on a space station.

In 2016, the CNSA launched Tiangong 2, a second space lab. Finally, in 2021, the CNSA launched the first section of its new Tiangong space station, called *Tianhe*. This bus-size space station will be the command center and living quarters of the three-section space station, which is designed to house three taikonauts at a time.

For a country that started in the space

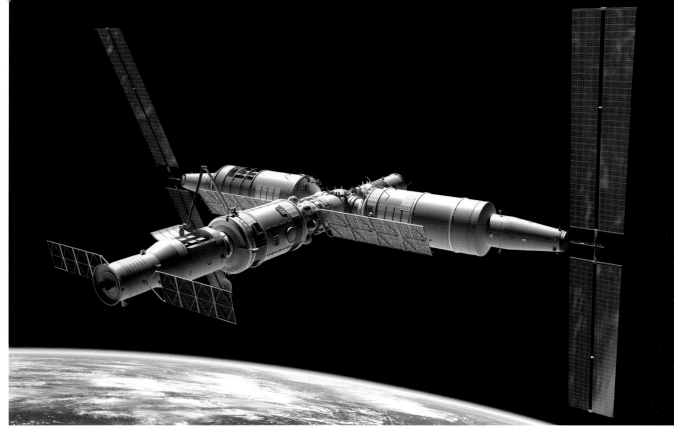

Chinese space station Tiangong orbiting Earth (artist's rendering).

race forty years later than the other leading nations, China has caught up quickly—and not just in the arena of human space exploration. In May 2021, engineers at the CNSA succeeded in landing a rover, named *Zhurong*, on Mars.

The US Response

What is the US response to China's success? For the most part, positive, but . . . cautious. When the CNSA's rover landed on Mars in 2021, Bill Nelson, the NASA Administrator, quickly congratulated the Chinese, saying, "The United States and the world look forward to the discoveries the *Zhurong* will make to advance humanity's knowledge of the Red Planet."

Later that day, speaking to the US Senate, Nelson noted that China is "a very aggressive competitor." Nelson was most likely informing the Senate that China was on its way to becoming a top player in space. In fact, some experts consider that the US and China are currently in a space race not unlike the one that existed between the US and Russia. Nelson has said, "I wish China were a partner with us, like the Russians have been."

NASA has been watching China's continued achievements in space exploration with great interest. After all, in

2019, China managed to do something that the US hasn't yet done: it delivered a robotic spacecraft to the far side of the Moon. This is not an easy task. It's extremely difficult to communicate with an object on the far side of the Moon, partly because the Moon blocks radio waves from Earth.

The knowledge to be gained from investigating that area of the Moon is priceless. Thankfully, China shared some of its data with the US. In a historic event, China and NASA collaborated on valuable research about the Moon. The US gave China information on its lunar orbiter satellite, and China shared the coordinates of its Chang'e 4 lander. The US was able to capture pictures of the lander shortly after it connected with the Moon's surface.

Then, in December 2023, NASA researchers were given permission to apply for access to lunar rocks and soil China retrieved from its Oceanus Procellarum site. NASA is eager to study these samples as they are from an area of the Moon that the US has not yet visited.

You might be wondering how NASA got around the Wolf Amendment. The answer is that the agency *can* work with China as long as it certifies to Congress that there's no way the project involves people in China who abuse human rights or steal trade secrets. The Federal Bureau of Investigation (FBI) checks to make absolutely sure that's the case.

Looking Ahead—Working Together?

Could these collaborations signal future cooperation between the US and China on space exploration? It's too early to tell, but China did sign the OST and participates with the US and other countries on the UN's Committee on the Peaceful Uses of Outer Space. These encouraging steps might be nudged along with help from a multinational organization called the International Space Exploration Coordination Group, in which the space agencies of the US, China, and seventeen other countries meet to share space-related information and plans. This is certainly a hopeful sign for cooperation!

On Expedition 1, the very first mission to the ISS, Bill Shepherd learned, "If we're going to go beyond LEO to the Moon, to Mars, the only way we're going to do that is to do it together." International treaties, norms, and accords are setting expectations for getting along with each other.

It is especially important to do that in low Earth orbit, because an increasing number of countries are placing satellites there. Let's look next at satellites and where they orbit.

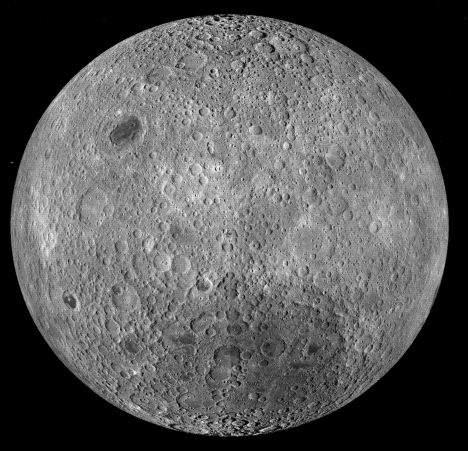

Top, image of the far side of the Moon, the side not visible from Earth; *bottom*, image of the Moon as we see it from Earth.

CHAPTER 6

Satellites and Where to Find Them

NASA's Earth-observing fleet of satellites.

Now seems like a good time to stop and discuss another topic that is very important in space: satellites. Let's start with a definition.

NASA defines a satellite as a "moon, planet or machine that orbits a planet or star." For the purposes of this book, we focus on satellites that are human-made objects placed into orbit around the Earth to gather and transmit information.

There are many types of satellites:

- meteorological satellites that gather data about Earth's climate and weather patterns
- navigation satellites that provide data for the Global Positioning System (GPS)
- communication satellites for computers, phones, and televisions
- cameras that take images of deep space for research
- cameras that take pictures of Earth to learn more about how our planet works
- military satellites
- and many more

It is difficult to imagine life without satellites. They help us communicate, make plans ahead of time based on weather conditions, find an address where we've never been, and find our way when we get lost.

Where Can You Find Satellites?

Low Earth orbit (LEO) is the perfect place for satellites (as well as space stations) because it is near Earth. That makes it relatively easy to launch satellites and have them achieve a stable orbit for a reasonable cost. While every satellite is different, most of them will hopefully stay in orbit for ten to fifteen years or more. That is, unless something happens to shift their orbit, like a collision or the failure of the satellite.

Finally, LEO allows for reliable monitoring from Earth and is cost-effective for maintenance visits, if needed. All these advantages make LEO an attractive area for satellites for both governments and commercial businesses.

Many new businesses are making their own satellites and launching them into LEO, which you'll read more about in Chapter 11 ("Howdy, Partners").

As the demand for satellites in LEO increases, private companies are pouring money into technology that is making them more efficient, longer lasting, and smaller. And as the size of satellites shrinks, costs decrease—after all, it costs less and takes less energy to launch a smaller satellite than a larger one. Lower prices make satellites more accessible for commercial companies to create and launch their own.

How Big Is a Satellite?

Satellites come in all shapes and sizes. Older satellites, those that were placed in orbit prior to 2006, tend to be larger because the technology wasn't available to reduce their size while maintaining their functionality. When scientists began working on the nanoscale—with objects whose size is measured in billionths of a meter—they were able to create amazingly small, powerful satellites. These are called CubeSats.

CubeSats are among the smallest satellites in space, and the most numerous.

Example of a CubeSat design.
These are satellites commonly used for science and exploration.

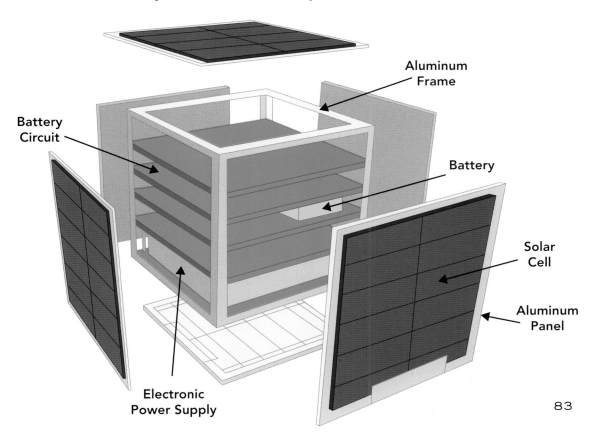

Battery Circuit

Aluminum Frame

Battery

Solar Cell

Aluminum Panel

Electronic Power Supply

Sixty Starlink broadband data satellites stacked atop a Falcon 9 rocket.

They are 10 centimeters by 10 centimeters by 10 centimeters, but can be joined into groups of two, three, or ten for a larger satellite. (Not sure how big a CubeSat is? Get out your ruler and draw a cube 10 cm x 10 cm x 10 cm, or 4 inches on each side.)

CubeSats can be deployed from land-based rocket launchers or in space via the ISS. They have revolutionized how humans use space. CubeSats provide detailed photographs of the planet to study weather, agriculture, geography, and more. They relay text messages from one area of the planet to another and keep information flow-ing via the Internet and television. Per-haps most importantly, CubeSats cost much less to launch into space than large satellites.

SmallSats, like the ones used in SpaceX's Starlink, are larger than CubeSats—about the size of a living room sofa—and can be linked together to form a very large satellite system. These are sometimes called satellite constellations or sky trains.

At the other end of the size spec-trum are huge satellites such as Blue-Birds, which are being constructed by a company called AST SpaceMobile. The solar array of a test prototype for one of these behemoths spanned 693 square feet. If they succeed, these mammoth satellites could serve as cell towers in the sky, providing direct satellite-to-smartphone communications services worldwide. The downside is that objects this large reflect light onto Earth. The prototype, BlueWalker 3, is one of the twenty brightest objects in the night sky.

Reducing the cost of sending satellites into space is great news for companies or countries looking to expand there. Yet the area of low Earth orbit is finite, meaning it has a defined area that cannot be expanded. With all the satellites and spacecraft, the Hubble Space Telescope, China's Tiangong space station, and the ISS—plus space debris—LEO is very crowded and getting more cramped every year. You'll learn more about this in Chapter 7 ("Bumper Cars in Space").

Satellites provide important information in the form of Global Positioning System (GPS) and weather data, communication platforms for cellular phones and computers, and scientific and military data. Life on Earth now depends on this information, and interruptions disrupt daily life. Imagine being unable to access the Internet, for example. This would be a significant disturbance for many people on the planet.

Light trails created by satellites on an astronomical photograph.

Dark and Quiet Skies

No matter their size, satellites can be seen from Earth when they're illuminated by the sun. Artificial objects like satellites and huge pieces of space debris appear as streaks of light in photographs, covering or distorting images of celestial bodies. Not surprisingly, astronomers are concerned that human-made sources of light can affect their research. They have even been fooled, tracking what they thought was shifting light from a star that turned out to be a lunar probe.

Artificially lit objects also distract humans on Earth from observing the splendor of planets, the Moon, and stars.

To try to limit the problem, SpaceX has developed "brightness mitigation" proposals. One of these is to mount sun visors that block sunlight from being reflected off the bottom of satellites. Another method would involve attaching mirrors to scatter light away from Earth. There is also the possibility of constructing satellites from nonreflective material. But it remains to be seen how widely adopted these proposals will be and how successful they are at keeping the sky dark and quiet.

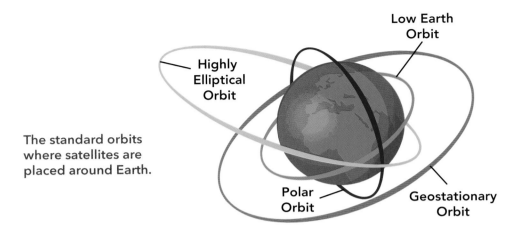

The standard orbits where satellites are placed around Earth.

Highly Elliptical Orbit

Low Earth Orbit

Polar Orbit

Geostationary Orbit

LEO Is Not the Only Option

As more and more satellites are placed into position around the Earth and low Earth orbit becomes more and more crowded, you might ask whether LEO is the only viable location for them. The answer is No. There are several different orbits around the planet that are easily accessible from Earth, and all are great for satellites.

In low Earth orbit, a satellite can travel along any path. This allows for many different routes for individual satellites.

The flexibility of movement and closeness, or proximity, to the Earth make LEO the best place for satellites that are viewing or mapping the surface of the Earth. There they can take the highest-resolution photographs. Objects in LEO travel at speeds of around 4.85 miles (7.8 km) per second and orbit the Earth about every ninety minutes. This means

Too Much of a Good Thing?

Some government officials, military leaders, and businesspeople are concerned about the possibility of a dire scenario in which telecommunications are abruptly cut off. How could this happen? As of 2024, SpaceX had about 5,400 satellites in the sky. These Starlink satellites accounted for more than 50 percent of all active satellites, and the company has announced plans to deliver 42,000 more in the next several years. Amazon projects that it will launch thousands as well, though far fewer than SpaceX. Together, they could provide worldwide Internet connections—a boon to underserved portions of the globe.

If a catastrophic accident occurred at Starlink headquarters, though, communications could be lost. Or the company could shut down a portion of its satellites. In fact, SpaceX CEO Elon Musk already has. During the war between Ukraine and Russia, he temporarily prevented Ukrainian soldiers from accessing military data. As a result, some countries are wary of relying on a single source for communications.

that they orbit Earth approximately sixteen times a day.

LEO is not the best place, however, for telecommunications satellites, or ones that relay information to and from transmitters and receivers. Telecommunication satellites are used by television, radio, Internet, telephone, and military organizations to send and receive information. Most telecommunication satellites are placed in geostationary orbit (GEO).

Geostationary orbit begins at 22,236 miles (35,786 km) above the Earth's surface. Satellites in GEO orbit the Earth around the equator and travel about 1.86 miles (3 km) per second, almost mimicking the speed of the Earth's rotation. They are said to be in a "fixed," or stationary, orbit, which allows them to always remain in practically the same place above Earth.

A satellite in GEO can be easily tracked from locations on the Earth's surface, which means that information is constantly provided in an accurate manner. Since these satellites are so much higher above Earth, fewer are needed to cover the entire surface. For now, there is less crowding in GEO. However, as the number of satellites being launched continues to grow, this situation promises to change in the future.

Satellites are also found in medium Earth orbit (MEO), which is located between LEO and GEO. MEO satellites behave like LEO satellites in that they can be found in any orbit around the Earth and are not limited to a fixed orbit like the GEO satellites. Most satellites in MEO are used for navigation, determining position on the planet. The satellites that make up the Global Positioning System (GPS), used by cellular phones and navigation apps, are located in MEO.

Satellites in polar orbit are in a nearly circular orbital path that is perpendicular to the equator. They travel over the South Pole, cross the equator around noon local time, and continue traveling

Hello! Can You Hear Me?

When you want to listen to music on the radio, you tune in to a station that has call letters to identify it, and a particular frequency of radio waves—say, 105.5 megahertz. But there are a limited number of frequencies, and therefore radio stations, available in the world. If two stations in the same location try to broadcast on frequencies that are too close together, they interfere with each other, like two people talking at the same time.

Your favorite station gets to use its frequency thanks to two organizations. The International Telecommunication Union (ITU), which is part of the United Nations, follows a complex but cooperative process to manage the ranges of frequencies around the world so they don't overlap. Then, within each country, another agency assigns a particular frequency to each station. In the United States, the Federal Communications Commission (FCC) does the job.

Satellites also use radio waves to communicate. To reach low Earth orbit and geostationary orbit, they need the high end of radio wave frequencies, and there's a limited number of these as well. On top of that, satellites need to use very specific frequencies so the signals hit the right satellite instead of others in the neighborhood. The International Telecommunication Union coordinates signals for satellites just as it does for radio stations.

So many private companies are placing satellites in LEO that the process might change. Still, this is a handy method for dividing up limited communications real estate, especially since countries around the world have agreed to it.

up to the North Pole. Each satellite in polar orbit continues this circular path, orbiting the Earth fifteen times a day so that it can view the entire surface during a twenty-four-hour cycle. Polar orbiting satellites are used for weather and mapping purposes.

Keeping an Eye on Things

The Space Surveillance Network (SSN) is operated by the US Space Force. It is a huge group of ground- and space-based sensors that track every human-made object that orbits Earth. The SSN works around the clock, every single day, to keep accurate positions on all trackable objects in space. It maintains close connections with commercial entities that are also tracking objects and routinely communicates with them to verify their data.

If one object appears to be on a collision course with another, that object is tracked closely. If possible, the two entities that own the objects are notified. If it is a piece of debris that might collide with an object, then the owner of the object is given advance notice so that it can possibly move its satellite or spacecraft.

You can keep track of the movements of satellites, observable debris, and other objects in real time, too. Take a look at Wayfinder in "Further Reading, Viewing, and Doing" at the back of this book.

Collisions in Space

It makes sense that objects orbiting at high speeds in the same area will, on occasion, collide. Imagine two cars slamming into each other at a very high speed. The cars are dented and broken, and bits of metal, glass, and plastic are strewn across the road. The same thing happens when two satellites collide: large debris fields are created. In space, debris fields can stay in place for days, months, or years. Bits of debris travel as fast as the satellites themselves and can be deadly. How would it feel if a piece of debris the size of a golf ball or even a grain of sand hit you going twice the speed of sound? Let's just say it would hurt. A lot.

Now imagine that piece hitting a satellite or a spacecraft. The impact could have devastating results. Space debris is a big problem. So big, in fact, that we've dedicated an entire chapter to explaining it.

Next up: What, if anything, can be done about space debris?

CHAPTER 7

Bumper Cars in Space

DEBRIS

Space debris (not to scale)
in low Earth orbit (artist's rendering).

Take Cover!

On November 15, 2021, just after 7 a.m. GMT, astronauts on the International Space Station were awakened early with the order to "take refuge" immediately. Unexpectedly, the ISS would be passing very close to a large area of space debris. At first NASA didn't know where the debris had come from.

But at that moment, the source didn't matter. Time was of the essence, as even one small bit of space debris could create enough damage to endanger the crew. NASA instructed the astronauts to institute their emergency protocol and immediately head to their spacecraft, on the chance that a collision would mean they needed to leave the space station.

The seven astronauts on board the ISS quickly donned their space suits and headed to their respective transport craft. The astronauts remained safely in their spacecraft for two hours, standing ready to undock immediately if necessary.

Fortunately, spacecraft are always docked at the ISS in case of an emergency. The astronauts remained in their transports until Mission Control gave them permission to return to the ISS. Normal work was somewhat disrupted, as the astronauts needed to stay near the spacecraft docking because the ISS passed near the debris field every ninety minutes. Finally, around 2:30 p.m., seven and a half hours after the initial debris appeared, the astronauts were able to return to their normal duties.

"Thanks for a crazy but well-coordinated day. We really appreciated all the situational awareness you gave us," said NASA astronaut Mark Vande Hei. He relayed this in a message to NASA's mission control during a check-in marking the end of the astronauts' day, adding, "it was certainly a great way to bond as a crew."

Out of Nowhere

Every day, NASA and Roscosmos strictly monitor a "pizza box"-shaped area around the ISS for dangerous objects and solar storms that might affect the space station. This "safety perimeter" is an area approximately 15 miles (25 km) around the space station and half a mile (three-fourths of a kilometer) above and below. Should any danger to the ISS appear within the safety perimeter, such as a piece of debris or a wayward satellite, Mission Control instructs the astronauts to fire the rockets on the ISS and move it to avoid a collision. Why didn't this happen? How could Mission Control possibly have missed this giant area of space debris?

They didn't miss it. The debris field wasn't there the day before. Around 7 a.m., about an hour after the astronauts woke up on November 15, the debris appeared out of nowhere. A few seconds earlier, the Russians had conducted an anti-satellite (ASAT) weapon test and blown up one of their own satellites. While the satellite was not in orbit right next to the ISS, its debris field reached into the normal orbital path of the ISS.

A. The ISS, carrying seven astronauts, sat in orbit approximately 248 miles (400 km) from the Earth. In orbit slightly above the ISS was Cosmos 1408, a defunct Russian spy satellite.

B. Russia conducted an ASAT weapon test that blew up Cosmos 1408 over Russian territory. The blast produced 1,500 pieces of debris traveling 17,500 mph in orbit 300 miles from Earth.

C. ISS astronauts were told to seek refuge in their transport craft because of the sudden appearance of the debris field, which passed by the ISS every 90 minutes for another seven and a half hours.

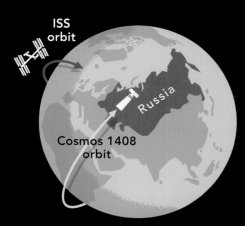

ISS orbit

Cosmos 1408 orbit

Russia

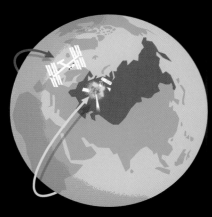

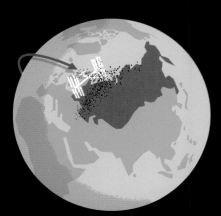

These orbits are approximations for illustrative purposes and should not be considered the actual orbits.

Why had Russia exploded their satellite? Most likely it was because it was old and no longer in service. This Russian satellite, Cosmos 1408, had been orbiting Earth since 1982. Designed to gather electronic signals information, Cosmos 1408 had long since stopped working. Still, exploding a 4,400-pound (2,000-kilogram) satellite with a bomb seemed excessive. The explosion initially created a massive debris field of more than 1,500 individual trackable pieces, each one capable of causing severe damage to the ISS and the astronauts inside.

Space Debris Is a BIG Deal

NASA defines space debris as "any human-made object in orbit around the Earth that no longer serves a useful function. Such debris includes nonfunctional spacecraft, abandoned launch vehicle stages, and parts remaining from completed missions." Put simply, if an object doesn't work but still orbits the Earth, it is considered debris—or, more aptly, "space junk."

In 2018, Elon Musk even launched a red Tesla with the first SpaceX Falcon Heavy. The car lacked an engine but carried a mannequin named Starman wearing a space suit. It has escaped Earth's orbit and is probably circling our sun, as space junk.

No matter whether it's huge or minuscule, debris is becoming a big problem. As of 2023, the Space Surveillance Network was regularly tracking just over 35,000 pieces of space debris. That amounts to more than 11,500 tons of useless stuff in LEO.

Some debris pieces are too small to have a digital imprint, but scientists use math to create estimates of the total number, which continues to increase. Computer estimates in December 2023 counted the number of objects that are larger than a softball (10 cm) at greater than 36,500; objects measuring between 1 and 10 centimeters at one million; and objects between 1 millimeter and 1 centimeter at 130 million.

Space reaches across hundreds of trillions of miles. What's the harm in having millions of bits of old junk floating around up there? The problem is that debris in orbit can collide with and damage or disable active spacecraft and satellites. Those collisions, in turn, create more debris, which then creates more collisions. It's a never-ending cycle, and one that is getting worse. Especially revealing is Privateer's website (wayfinder.privateer.com), which allows you to see the number of satellites in orbit and to filter in or out all the known debris.

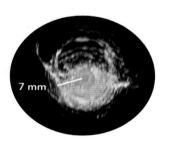

Damage to the glass cupola of the ISS was caused by a tiny piece of space debris.

7 mm

Itty-Bitty Fragments Can Be Lethal

It's very likely that every object in space has experienced some sort of debris impact. That includes the International Space Station. In May 2016, a bit of debris no larger than a flake of paint caused a 7-millimeter indentation in the space station's cupola window. British astronaut Tim Peake, who pointed out the indentation while on board the ISS, said, "This is the chip in one of our cupola windows; glad it is quadruple glazed!"

Impacts like this happen all the time. When the US was using space shuttles on a regular basis, their windows were constantly being replaced due to hits from small debris. A 1-centimeter paint chip, no bigger than a human fingernail, zooming through space can inflict the same amount of damage as a 550-pound object traveling 60 miles per hour on Earth. Space engineers understand this and plan for it so the ISS stays in good working order.

But how can something so tiny carry such a powerful punch?

Most space junk is in low Earth orbit, where many satellites are found. Each piece of debris, regardless of its size, travels between 17,500 and 18,000 mph. That's more than twenty-three times the speed of sound.

How Fast Is the Speed of Sound?

The speed of sound is dependent upon the density of the air, which means that it varies with temperature and pressure. The denser the air, the lower the speed of sound. An object traveling at the speed of sound is said to be traveling at Mach 1. At sea level on a standard day, Mach speed is approximately 761 miles per hour. But for most aerospace calculations, the number is 767 mph under standard temperature and pressure conditions.

Passenger planes do not fly at Mach speeds. Instead, they fly much slower. For example, a Boeing 747 plane flies at approximately 570 mph. You would know if your plane travels at Mach 1 or higher, because you would hear a gigantic BOOM! That is known as a sonic boom.

An image of the large amounts of debris found floating in space at GEO (geosynchronous orbit).

What Is an ASAT?

An anti-satellite (ASAT) weapon is a land-based missile that has been launched into space with the express purpose of destroying a satellite. In the case of the November 15, 2021, incident, the Russians launched a PL-19 Nudol missile into space. This is an anti-ballistic missile originally designed to protect Russia from a nuclear attack on the Earth. Now these missiles are being used as anti-satellite weapons to take down outdated satellites in low Earth orbit.

The PL-19 Nudol was shot from a mobile launcher at the Plesetsk Cosmodrome, which is about 500 miles north of Moscow. The armed missile headed directly into space and exploded upon contact with the targeted satellite.

Russian engineers had tested their ASAT system several times in 2021 but did not blow up a satellite. This time, however, Cosmos 1408 was destroyed, resulting in thousands of tiny pieces of debris.

Russia is not the only country with the capability of launching ASAT missiles. The United States, China, and India possess ASAT missile systems and have tested them, each adding to the debris orbiting in LEO.

By the end of 2022, the UN approved a resolution encouraging countries not to carry out ASAT tests. One hundred fifty-five countries voted for it, excluding China, Russia, and seven others. By 2023, the US and thirty-six other countries declared they would no longer conduct direct-ascent ASAT tests.

The FIRST Piece of Space Debris

On October 4, 1957, the Soviet Union launched Sputnik, the first ever human-made satellite, into space. Sputnik maintained its orbit around the Earth and signaled the start of the Space Age. Interestingly, Sputnik was also the very first piece of space debris. It operated successfully for three weeks, sending information back to the Soviets about the layers of the Earth's atmosphere. It then stopped functioning but remained in orbit for a total of ninety-two days, until it finally slowed enough that its orbit degraded, causing it to fall back into Earth's atmosphere and burn up. Since Sputnik was not functioning for most of those ninety-two days, NASA considered it space debris.

A REALLY BIG Piece of Space Junk?

In Chapter 2 ("Seeking a Lunar Perspective") we mentioned that the ISS will probably reach the end of its life in 2030. What will happen to this massive 460-ton home in the sky?

NASA and its partner space agencies have known from the beginning that the ISS cannot make an uncontrolled reentry into Earth's atmosphere. America's first space station, Skylab, which was one-sixth the size of the ISS, did just that in 1979, spreading debris in western Australia. If the ISS were left to deorbit on its own, it could bump into satellites on its way down and damage or disable them. Without propulsion or a steering mechanism, there is no way to predict where the ISS would land on Earth.

NASA's current plan is to contract with a company to build a Deorbit Vehicle that will return the ISS to Earth. The goal is to submerge the ISS in an uninhabited area of the South Pacific Ocean, known as Point Nemo. That is the only way, an advisor warned, "to avert a catastrophe." We hope that Congress agrees and funds this project, which will cost an estimated one billion dollars.

If an object slows down, its orbit will degrade, and it will eventually re-enter Earth's atmosphere and burn up or crash into the ocean or on the ground. In the meantime, the debris field from Russia's 2021 ASAT test may continue to be a problem for the ISS, as it may conflict on occasion with its orbit. Since bits of the debris are very small and light, they will take many, many years to slow down and fall into Earth's atmosphere. That means that Mission Control needs to be aware of the position of the field every time the ISS passes by, and the astronauts may need to continually maneuver around it.

Now, imagine two pieces of junk that have not slowed and are hurtling toward each other at Mach 23—twenty-three times the speed of sound. Their collision could smash each piece into many more, even smaller bits.

Donald Kessler, a senior scientist at NASA in the 1990s, theorized that LEO could get so congested with debris and other objects that a cascade of collisions could result. Debris might continually collide, producing more debris and so on, until the danger to working satellites is so great that LEO becomes unusable. This scenario is known as the Kessler Syndrome. Although there is much debate, some experts believe the Kessler Syndrome has already begun.

An astronomer described the possible future of satellite traffic in LEO this way: "It's going to be like an interstate highway, at rush hour in a snowstorm with everyone driving much too fast. Except there are multiple interstate highways crossing each other with no stoplights."

What can the spacefaring community do to avert this catastrophic outcome?

Outer Space Treaty to the Rescue?

Russia's explosion of Cosmos 1408, which we described at the beginning of this chapter, contributed innumerable pieces of dangerous junk to this blizzard of debris. And people around the world were livid. The US called the act "reckless." Britain condemned Roscosmos's "complete disregard for the security, safety, and sustainability of space." Despite their fury, though, everyone's hands were tied. They could complain, but that's all.

The reason is that the ASAT test may have been irresponsible, but it was not illegal. While the slogan "Don't Mess with Texas" means you'd better not toss so much as a straw onto a Texas state highway, there's no law against

Floating space debris orbiting Earth consists of old satellites, rocket parts, and pieces of metal (artist's rendering).

littering space with spent rockets, stray wrenches, or shards of metal.

This might come as a surprise when you look at the Outer Space Treaty. Several articles could appear to ban blowing up satellites in the orbit of the ISS.

For instance, countries should

- let each other know of hazards that might threaten astronauts (Article V),
- control the objects they send into space (Article VIII),
- show "due regard" for each other by keeping everyone's best interests in mind (Article IX), and
- check with each other before doing something that might cause harm (Article IX).

You might think that, taken together, these requirements in the OST would not allow countries to scatter junk that puts people, satellites, and space stations at risk. Or if they did, either accidentally or on purpose, they'd have to warn them. Yet Russia did not abide by any of these provisions when it blew up Cosmos 1408.

How have Russia and other countries that have conducted ASAT tests been able to ignore the Outer Space Treaty? The answer is that they haven't ignored it. The OST doesn't say anything about debris. It sets out important general principles, but not the specifics of when or how they should be applied.

Still, the OST has been useful. It has spawned additional treaties, two of which might help address the problem of space debris someday and help keep conditions in space sustainable. These are the Liability Convention and the Registration Convention. ("Convention" in this case is another word for treaty.)

Who Caused That Collision? How Do You Know?

In 1972, the United Nations filled in some missing details in Article VII of the Outer Space Treaty by adopting the Liability Convention. This treaty says that figuring out who covers the cost of a collision depends on where the damage occurs—on the ground or up in space.

If an accident harms something *on Earth*, the country that launched the spacecraft has to pay for the damage. It doesn't matter how it happens. It doesn't even matter if the country that launched it didn't cause the problem. If you send it up and it falls down, you pay. This means that countries that launch objects into space need to check them very carefully to be sure they're good to go up—and stay up.

The situation is different, though, if an object *in space* is hurt. The Liability Convention says that launching countries have to pay for damage there only if the crash is their fault. It might not make complete sense but it's the law. Not only that but the treaty doesn't define the word "fault."

Still, the first part of the Liability Convention came in handy just six years after it was ratified when a Soviet satellite powered by a very small nuclear reactor lost power and abruptly de-orbited. It broke apart upon reentry into Earth's atmosphere, spewing radioactive waste over 120,000 square km of northern Canada. Pointing to the Liability Convention, Canada negotiated with the USSR, which agreed to pay for part of the cleanup. The deal cost the Soviets about three million Canadian dollars.

Remember to Wear Your Name Tag

In 1974, the UN piggybacked on Article VIII of the OST to adopt the Registration Convention. This one requires countries to register everything they launch. In fact, they have to list it in two places: a database in their home country and also with the UN's Office for Outer Space Affairs. That way if objects collide, space agencies will know who owns the objects, and they can go after

Space Debris in Your Backyard

What could you do if debris falls from space and hits your house? The OST and the Liability Convention say you should call your national government. Your country can then file a complaint, like an insurance claim, against the government that launched the piece of space junk. Eventually, you would probably get reimbursed for the damage.

The chance of getting bombarded by an object from space is minuscule, but it can happen. In 2024, a two-pound chunk from a battery that was attached to a cargo pallet crashed through the roof and two floors of a home in Florida. The debris had probably been tossed from the ISS three years earlier. Fortunately, no one was hurt, but the owner wanted someone to cover the cost of repairing his house. And that situation quickly got complicated.

The battery was probably owned by NASA and the pallet by a different agency. Yet, it wasn't immediately clear which country launched them. This book was printed before all the facts were known and the issues resolved.

The link in this QR code will show you how space debris might look as it falls from the sky.

them—or at least point fingers to figure out who's at fault.

Registering objects launched into space is a great idea. But it works only as long as the objects remain whole. Once they're smashed to bits, it can be hard to figure out who owns which sliver. Also, some countries and companies simply don't follow the rules.

The first collision between satellites from different countries occurred in 2009 when a defunct Russian satellite, Cosmos 2251, struck a working satellite, Iridium 33, that was owned by an American company. The impact immediately scattered about 2,000 chunks of debris large enough to be tracked, plus thousands of tinier ones, throughout LEO.

Some of the pieces have burned up in Earth's atmosphere. Hundreds of others could remain in orbit for at least a century.

Who will have to pay if debris from Iridium 33 or Cosmos 2251 ruins another working satellite someday? No one knows. Neither the US nor Russia had registered those satellites, even though both countries had signed the Registration Convention. We'll say more about rule-breakers in Chapter 12 ("Who's In Charge Around Here?").

If there's a big smash-up in the sky, space lawyers will be spending a lot of time figuring out how to get someone to cover the costs.

What Can We Do About Space Debris?

Clearly, the OST is not the right vehicle for getting countries to deal with their space junk. A group of scientists at the NASA Jet Propulsion Lab are so concerned that they're calling for another international treaty, which would finally make it illegal to scatter debris. As we mentioned, 155 countries approved a UN resolution discouraging ASAT tests, which thirty-seven countries have banned. By 2024, forty-four space companies—not including SpaceX—pledged to follow it. But a resolution isn't a treaty.

Meanwhile the number of collisions keeps rising, resulting in more and more space debris being created. Is there anything to be done?

There are currently three major methods for tackling the problem of space debris:

- manage space traffic to reduce the chance of collisions,
- haul off the debris that is already in space,
- limit the amount of additional debris in the future.

These methods involve complex technological developments and delicate national and international negotiations.

Managing Traffic in Space

The first step is to track the debris. This process is often called "situational space awareness." Knowing where space debris is located at all times helps companies and nations understand the danger to their satellites and space stations. If they are notified of an impending collision, they might be able to move the objects into a different orbit to prevent damage. Such maneuvers, though, can be costly in terms of fuel, time, and loss of service.

Thus, tracking space debris has become big business. The US, Russia, France, Germany, and Japan, among other countries, have set up organizations and companies to monitor objects in space and predict close calls.

Leo Labs is one of those companies. Founded by physicist, engineer, and former astronaut Dr. Ed Lu and electrical engineer Dr. Dan Ceperly, Leo Labs uses sixty-two ground-based radars to track more than 250,000 pieces of debris in low Earth orbit down to the size of a nut and bolt. Leo Labs offers a "collision avoidance service" for companies that subscribe to its product. This system alerts a company if its satellite is about to experience a head-on crash or a glancing collision. Leo Labs works with SpaceX and the US Department of Defense to help keep them informed about space debris.

Leo Labs was one of the first companies to notice the debris from the Russian ASAT test in 2021 that we described at the beginning of this chapter. It notified NASA, which confirmed the debris with government space debris tracking systems. This quick action helped the astronauts take cover in time to avoid a possible collision.

Many other companies are developing space tracking capabilities, including one in Belgium that is developing technology to find debris as small as an inch. Some companies are sharing information, too. AstriaGraph, a public-private

Stash or Burn?

Deorbiting space junk so it burns up in the atmosphere might seem like the simplest way to dispose of it. Sizzle! Poof! It's gone. But this process might create air pollution that affects Earth's climate. In addition, scientists have recently learned that burning might also pollute the stratosphere.

What about submerging pieces in the ocean that are so large they won't burn up? The best site to stash junk on Earth is Point Nemo, a spot in the South Pacific that is so remote, the closest human habitat is the ISS. Here, though, scientists worry about effects on the marine environment.

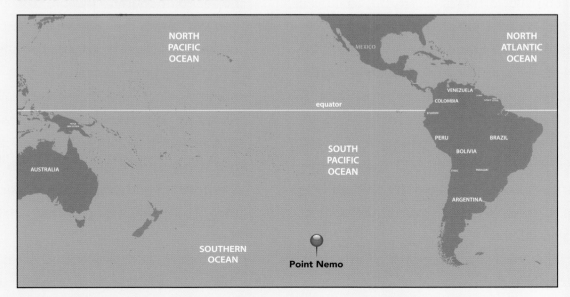

Point Nemo, the most remote location on Earth, known as the "spacecraft cemetery."

partnership created by Dr. Moriba Jah, a space dynamics scientist at the University of Texas, maintains a huge database of objects floating in space. This system is crowd-sourced, which means that anyone can access the information and add to it, even someone with a telescope in their own backyard.

The aim of AstriaGraph is to develop an understanding of where each and every object placed in space exists. Supercomputers store and analyze the data so that the information is useful to companies that want to place a new satellite or keep their existing satellite safe.

Tracking is a great tool, but is there a way to get rid of the space debris?

Clean It Up!

Governments and companies are working to develop ways to remove debris. Mechanical arms or Earth-based lasers could nudge junk away from the orbits of space stations and satellites. Or pieces of debris could be slowed down so they burn up in Earth's atmosphere. A third way of handling debris is to move pieces into a proposed "graveyard orbit," more than 22,000 miles above Earth—above GEO—where the objects are a great distance from other operating satellites.

Here are a few examples of attempts to capture debris:

- Astroscale, a Japanese company, is working with ESA on refueling, removal, and overall traffic management of the satellites in space. As of February 2024, Astroscale launched a mission designed to perform an RPO (rendezvous and proximity operation) maneuver next to a piece of debris. If this mission is successful, it will pave the way for the next step of capturing the debris and moving it to a nonoperational area.
- ClearSpace, a Swiss company, aims to develop a satellite with four autonomous arms to grab debris and bring it down to de-orbit. This might not be ready for testing until at least 2025. ClearSpace is working with eight countries in ESA.
- Privateer, a US-based company, hopes to encourage people to see space as a fourth environment of the Earth, and to approach it with respect and planning so that objects being put into space can be safely removed when they cease to function. It also hopes to have a tracking system that will describe the position and orientation of each object to assist in its capture.

All of these methods sound pretty nifty. Who could object to tidying up space? After all, everyone benefits from a cleaner environment.

But cost is an issue. The United States, Russia, and China have left the most trash in space. How should the cost of removing it be shared? One suggestion is to provide incentives. Instead of a space race, hold a clean-up-space race. Any suggestions for prizes?

Less Is More

Ultimately, the best way to decrease space debris is for countries and companies to remove objects when they are no longer usable. This task is called debris mitigation. An example is Aeolus, a defunct satellite that the ESA maneuvered into low Earth orbit, where most of it burned up.

In 2009, the UN recommended guidelines to reduce debris, including

- limiting the release of rocket parts into Earth's orbit during launch,
- venting leftover fuel, and
- discharging batteries in end-stage satellites to reduce the risk of dangerous explosions.

Several countries—but not all—have adopted policies that their governments and businesses should follow to implement some—but not all—of the UN-recommended guidelines. The ESA, for example, launched a Zero Debris Charter in 2023, calling for no debris in orbits used by satellites, space stations, and other devices by 2030. US government agencies are also working to ensure that private companies limit debris. In 2023, the Federal Aviation Administration developed rules requiring various mechanisms, such as controlled reentry or using a "graveyard" orbit.

The Federal Communications Commission went even further. As we mentioned in Chapter 6 ("Satellites and Where to Find Them"), this agency regulates telecommunications frequencies for private companies launching satellites. Those companies were expected to keep their satellites in their designated orbits and, at the end of their life, dispose of them properly. But there was no way to really enforce these practices. That all changed on October 2, 2023. For the first time ever, the FCC issued a fine to a private company for failing to dispose of its defunct satellite properly.

DISH Network had a satellite in GEO that had reached the end of its mission. According to standard practice, the satellite needed to be boosted to the graveyard orbit, approximately 300 km above GEO. DISH filed a mitigation plan with the FCC saying that it would make this happen. The problem was that the satellite did not have enough fuel left to get that high. Instead, it was boosted only to 122 km above GEO. The FCC determined that this was too close to GEO and could "pose orbital debris concerns." In a groundbreaking decision, DISH was fined $150,000 by the FCC for failure to dispose of its satellite properly.

Is this fine the first step to a new US policy of regulating space debris more closely? Perhaps. In December 2023, the US Senate approved a bill to encourage the Commerce Department and NASA to take a closer look at debris in LEO. This Orbital Sustainability (ORBITS) Act calls for a list of potentially hazardous debris that should be removed and for instructions on how to carry out the removal. It remains to be seen if this bill will pass the US House of Representatives and be signed into law, but it is a start.

As you can see, there is no worldwide consensus on how to reduce space debris. The UN guidelines, as well as the guidelines of the Americans and the Europeans, are just that—etiquette guidelines. They are "norms of behavior," which you read about in Chapter 4 ("Play Nice!"). They're not required, or even widely agreed to. The conundrum that hangs over the world is how to find solutions that can be put into place before the Kessler Syndrome gets worse.

To Regulate or Not to Regulate? That Is a Question

US government agencies overseeing debris mitigation are in a bit of a quandary. They wish they could make companies follow rules to clean up after themselves and keep the space environment tidy. But they don't want to make the rules so tough that American companies pick up and move to other countries that don't require costly pollution controls.

Like a lot in politics, it's tricky to figure out the right balance between carrots and sticks—that is, between encouraging people to be neat, on the one hand, and punishing them for cluttering, on the other. You could hardly send a company into time-out for making a mess in space.

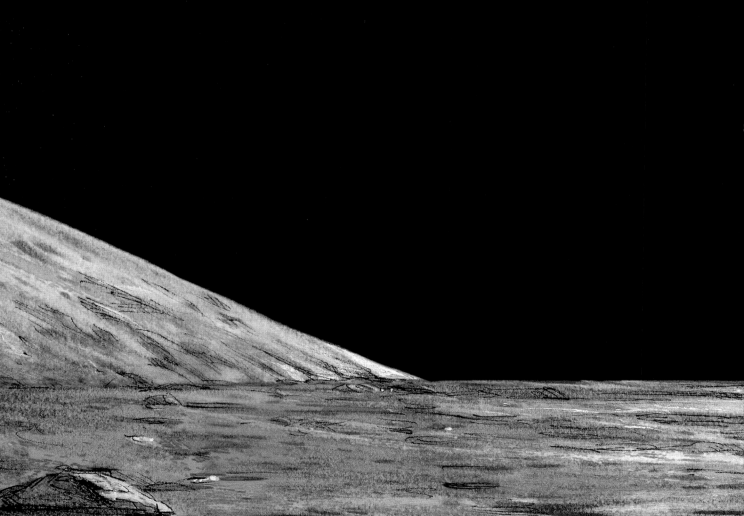

CHAPTER 8

Hey! Who Are You Looking At?

TECHNOLOGY IN SPACE

Just Taking Out the Trash?

With a giant roar, a huge column of flames, and billows of smoke, the Long March 3B rocket lifted off of the platform at Xichang Satellite Launch Center in southwestern China on October 24, 2021. Attached to the top of the three-stage booster was the Shijian-21 satellite.

Shijian-21 was headed to space to "test and verify space debris mitigation technologies." A few hours later, the satellite entered a planned orbit around the Earth. But unlike most satellites, Shijian-21 (SJ-21) did not remain there for very long.

Less than a week after SJ-21 entered a stable orbit, the US Space Command noticed something new. There was another object near SJ-21.

The Space Command assumed that this extra blip on their screen was an apogee kick motor (AKM), not an extra satellite. AKMs are sometimes used to provide extra power to "kick" the satellite into its final position. Normally, these are used once, and then discarded as debris. But that's not how this AKM behaved.

Over the next several weeks, SJ-21 and the AKM appeared to move about each other. First the satellite moved away from the AKM, then got closer, and then moved away again. No satellite and AKM had ever behaved in this way before.

What was going on?

The US was about to find out.

In December 2021, SJ-21 began moving toward a dead Chinese satellite, Compass G2. Compass G2 was considered debris because it had never worked properly. As the members of the US Space Force tracked the two satellites on their screens, they saw SJ-21 move alongside Compass G2.

Suddenly, on January 22, 2022, SJ-21 disappeared!

The abrupt disappearance of SJ-21 from the tracking maps caused more than a few raised eyebrows and sent many organizations on Earth scrambling to locate it.

The Space Command conducted a massive search, collecting radar data from many different satellite tracking sites. No one registered new debris. So SJ-21 hadn't been destroyed. Where was it? SJ-21 had docked with—or attached itself to—Compass G2. The now larger satellite began moving upward.

Apparently, SJ-21 was acting as a "space tugboat." It was towing the defunct Compass G2 to a higher orbit, to an area referred to as a satellite "graveyard."

Upon reaching the higher orbit, SJ-21 released Compass G2 and headed back to its original orbit within GEO. In effect, China had just taken out its trash.

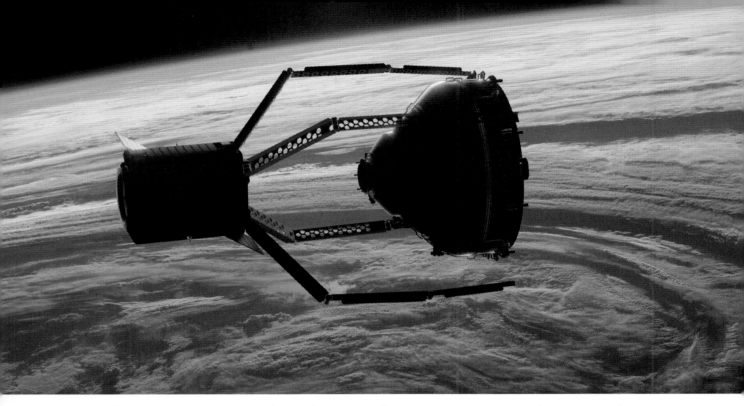

It is difficult to obtain imagery of a rendezvous and proximity operation (RPO) in space. This is an artist's rendering of a mission that was planned by ClearSpace to capture Europe's Vega launcher from orbit. As of April 2024, this mission has now been changed to capture the PROBA-1 satellite and together deorbit through Earth's atmosphere.

Relocating a Satellite Is Not Easy

So what really happened in GEO? Had the world just witnessed a new Chinese satellite capability? After much analysis of the satellite data, the US concluded the answer was yes. With SJ-21, China had a satellite that was "clearly capable of [conducting] close proximity operations, docking, and maneuver[ing]."

The act of one satellite approaching another is not a new capability. This maneuver, known as a rendezvous and proximity operation (RPO), has been performed by many different space agencies—NASA, ESA, Roscosmos, CSA, the Japan Aerospace Exploration Agency (JAXA), and others, as well as commercial companies. It is now considered a relatively routine operation.

So why did the movements made by China's satellite cause some concern among other countries? It might have been the unexpected maneuverability of SJ-21. Most satellites are launched, reach a stable position, and remain in place. If you could look up at a satellite in GEO, it would appear stationary, except for a

How Does a Spy Satellite Work?

Spy satellites provide signals intelligence, or SIGINT, to whoever owns them. They listen in on thousands of cell phone calls and search the Internet for terrorist activity.

The US has a class of spy satellites called Orion. These are owned by the National Reconnaissance Office (NRO). At least seven satellites are known to be a part of the Orion network. The one we describe here is NROL-44, which launched on December 10, 2020.

The NROL-44 satellite is huge! It weighs more than 5 tons and has a parabolic antenna that, when unfolded after placement in space, is as long as an American football field. Its job is to capture the information radiating from cell phone towers as people are using their phones. It can also pick up wireless Internet signals and track them to their place of origin.

How can it do this? The massive antenna picks up the information that radiates electronically from the cell phone towers. It's like a giant ear, listening to practically everything happening on the planet.

A United Launch Alliance (ULA) Delta IV Heavy rocket carrying the NROL-44 mission for the National Reconnaissance Office (NRO) lifts off from Space Launch Complex 37 at 8:09 p.m. (EST) on Dec. 10, 2020.

tiny wobble. SJ-21 was the exception. Its ease of movement was previously seen only in spacecraft, not satellites.

The fact that SJ-21 dragged the Compass G2 satellite in an elliptical course was also surprising. Normally, raising a satellite up to the graveyard area is done by moving directly upward.

By demonstrating this ability, China firmly established itself as a significant-presence in space. After all, the launch of SJ-21 was only one of fifty-five rockets that China sent into space in 2021.

Yet even with all these surprises, shouldn't the accomplishment of the Chinese have been celebrated? Relocating a dead satellite to the graveyard above GEO and returning to its original orbit is an amazing engineering feat and shows that it is possible for a country to responsibly remove its dead satellites from active areas of space—a goal of many spacefaring nations.

So why were the US and European countries still wary? It comes down to perspective.

Perspective Is Everything

The development of new technology is awe-inspiring, but it can also be controversial. For example, cellular phones allow us to communicate with people wherever they are, including in case of an emergency. But they also contain GPS chips that can be tracked. Some people might think that this tracking ability is an unacceptable invasion of privacy. Others might not care at all that their movements could be monitored. The difference is in how you look at things and what you value.

Let's apply that same reasoning to the SJ-21 satellite. Some portion of the international community applauded China's effort to clean up its mess in space. The fact that China's technology had the potential to reduce the tens of thousands of pieces of debris in space was positive. Yet the US perspective was different. The ability to move satellites was great, but it made the US wonder what else China might do with that ability. Would China restrict itself to moving only its own satellites, or would it consider moving satellites that belonged to others?

And if it did, what could other nations do about it?

That is the question that the US and other spacefaring countries were asking themselves.

While technology can be used to further science and expand horizons, it can

Robotic Satellite Technology for the US

Robotic technology to move satellites may be available in the US soon, too. The commercial aerospace company Northrop Grumman is developing a satellite servicing vehicle known as a Mission Extension Vehicle (MEV), which will be able to dock with a satellite in orbit. Once attached, the MEV will be able to move the satellite, changing its direction or boosting it to stay in orbit. Mission Robotic Vehicles (MRVs) will also be used to inspect and repair satellites. A Mission Refueling Pod (MRP) will provide new energy to a satellite to extend its life. If a satellite is not able to be repaired, the MEV would remove the dead satellite from its orbit and tow it to the graveyard.

also be used for military objectives. This is why every time one country demonstrates a new technology, others are probably quietly assessing its potential for military use.

This is a conundrum. How is it possible to tell if an achievement such as moving a satellite from one orbit to another should be celebrated for its amazing engineering or viewed as a possible threat to another country? It's all about perspective.

Peering Over Fences

Satellites do phenomenal things. As we've said above, they help with our everyday lives. And yet some of them also

perform activities that might be considered invasive. Think of a satellite being like a nosy neighbor peering over your fence. Watching you. Recording everything that you do.

This is our reality in today's world. Ask yourself: How is a satellite that is watching other countries any different from the surveillance camera at your local grocery store, or the camera at the intersection that flags you for running a red light? It's not, really.

Many countries own and use spy satellites. In fact, it is estimated that one-fifth of all satellites orbiting our planet are spy satellites and are owned by various militaries.

While these are supposed to be top secret, it is known that the US has a program with a company called United Launch Alliance to routinely launch secret payloads containing—among other items—spy satellites. These satellites are placed into orbit at specific altitudes to watch whatever the US wants to monitor. They are run exclusively by the military.

While the exact number of spy satellites is top secret and therefore not known to the public, it is believed that, as of 2023, the US may have 485 or more in orbit. The Russians have about seventy known spy satellites. The Chinese have just over sixty. But they aren't the only countries that have them.

Rendezvous and Proximity Operations

During an RPO, two objects in space will shift their positions to move very close to each other and even match orbits. These objects can be two satellites or a satellite and its AKM. During the RPO, the objects sometimes dock, or connect to each other physically. While connected, they can exchange information to update one of the satellites or extend its life; remove an outdated satellite from orbit; or perform refueling and maintenance procedures. RPOs occur often in space and are usually not a cause for concern.

Japan, Mexico, Colombia, Turkey, and many countries in Europe appear to each have as many as ten spy satellites. More countries continue to step into the spy satellite arena. It's safe to say that many countries are often peering over their neighbors' fences.

Military forces can also get information from commercial satellites. This ability can be very useful in case of a natural disaster or for tracking a ship that might be fishing illegally. But the situation gets complicated if one country believes that another one is using a commercial satellite to spy on it. If the spied-on country damages the satellite, that could harm civilians who need it to check the weather or chat with their friends. As a result, tensions could escalate.

Where Does That Leave Us?

Spying on other countries is done all the time by those countries that have satellites capable of doing so. The world's superpowers are super aware of the importance of space and of making sure their citizens stay safe and secure. Countries that have eyes in the sky can, and should, use their equipment in space to keep the peace. But will they? We hope so.

Let's move on from this heavy topic and lighten things up. Have you ever thought about going to space? Maybe as a tourist? If so, this next chapter will pique your interest. There are ways that people can fly to space without going through the lengthy, intense training to become an astronaut. At the present time, it does require a healthy bank account, though. . . .

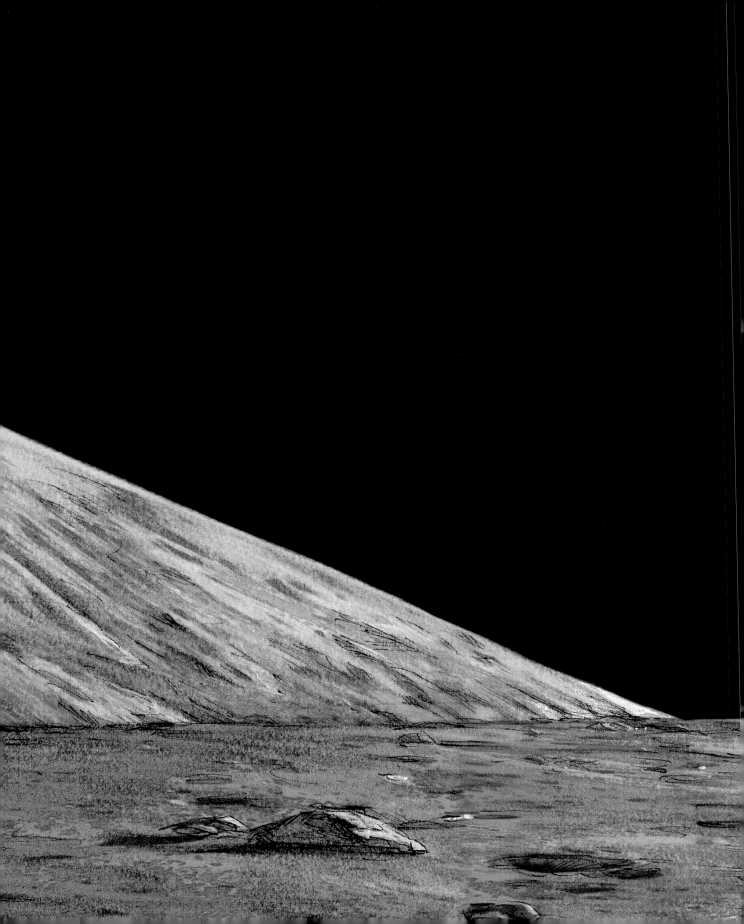

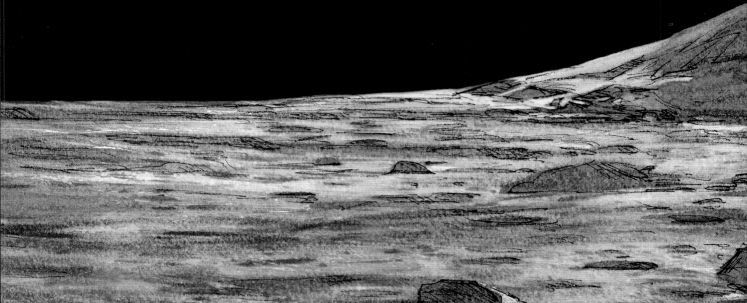

Inspiration4: Civilians in Space

"Are you ready?" the announcer called. "Super Bowl LV is under way!"

An estimated 96.4 million football fans watched the Tampa Bay Buccaneers face off against the Kansas City Chiefs on February 7, 2021. And many of them viewed the famous halftime commercials. One ad stood out from the rest. It opened with Celeste softly singing "Twinkle, twinkle, little star" as glimpses of a space suit floating in space came into view.

Was someone selling space gear? Stardust?

No. The narrator explained, "This fall, Inspiration4 launches as the first all-civilian mission. And you could be on board. Visit inpiration4.com for your chance to go to space."

With a donation to St. Jude Children's Research Hospital in Memphis, Tennessee, anyone could enter a sweepstakes to win a trip to space! Inspiration4, a new and little-known company, was looking for regular people—civilians—to go to space for three days.

"That's kind of an interesting opportunity," Chris Sembroski thought. He pulled out his phone and contributed $50. His best friend and about 70,000 other people entered the contest, too.

Sembroski's friend won! But he was unable to accept and turned his seat over to Chris. The friend knew that Chris would make a good astronaut. After all, Chris was an engineer, Air Force veteran, and Space Camp attendee and counselor where he learned about rocketry, life aboard the ISS, and gravity simulations. The sponsor of this adventure, a billionaire named Jared Isaacman, agreed, and Sembroski joined the team.

Isaacman hosted the contest because he believed that space should be open for everyone, not just astronauts. This excursion would be the first step toward his ultimate goal of "making humankind a multiplanetary species."

He bought all four seats on the Crew Dragon, a spacecraft built by SpaceX, and planned to give three away. Isaacman and Sembroski would each take one. The third seat went to St. Jude's employee, Hayley Arceneaux, a twenty-nine-year-old physician's assistant and former cancer patient with a prosthetic leg bone.

Isaacman held a competition on Twitter for the fourth seat. The winner was Dr.

Sian Proctor, a science educator, pilot, poet, and artist. She had also been a NASA astronaut finalist whose father helped track NASA's Apollo 11 flight.

Picking the crew was the easy part. Training would be more challenging.

For five and a half months, the novice space travelers trained up to sixty hours a week. Although the Crew Dragon was autonomous—meaning that software and ground control managed all operations—the crew needed to learn the mechanics of handling the craft, in case of an operational failure. To prepare for the rigors of their adventure, they flew in an airplane that executed up and down, parabolic maneuvers to simulate seconds of microgravity, and practiced water survival maneuvers. Testing their mental and physical endurance, they even climbed 4,400 feet up Mount Rainier in ice and snow.

On September 16, 2021, the foursome rocketed into space from Kennedy Space Center's historic pad 39A. It seemed appropriate that this momentous send-off should take place on the same pad NASA had used to launch the Apollo missions to the Moon and the first space shuttle, *Columbia*.

For three days, the Inspiration4 crew zoomed at 17,500 miles per hour, orbiting Earth almost fifty times, at about 365 miles (585 km) up. That's about 100 miles higher than the International Space Station. Once they got over their space-queasiness, they conducted experiments in microgravity, talked with patients at St. Jude's, took photographs of Earth from the Dragon's cupola, and figured out how to troubleshoot the leaky toilet.

After splashing down in the Atlantic Ocean near Cape Canaveral, the teammates were exhilarated. They had raised more than $200 million for St. Jude's. More importantly, they had made history as the first all-civilian crew in space. As their lead trainer said, "We're changing perceptions about who can go to space and how you can end up going to space."

Inspiration4 crew takes a selfie in the Crew Dragon cupola. *Left to right:* Jared Isaacman, Chris Sembroski, Sian Proctor, and *bottom right,* Hayley Arceneaux.

Private Citizens in Space

Inspiration4's Jared Isaacman, Chris Sembroski, Hayley Arceneaux, and Sian Proctor, the world's first all-civilian crew to orbit Earth, proved that ordinary people can live and work in space, at least for a short time.

Their trip was the first step toward opening up space to everyone. The ESA has hired John McFall, a Paralympian with a prosthetic lower leg, to join its ranks.

The Inspiration4 crew, though, were not the first civilians to hurtle into space. That honor goes to an American engineer named Charles Walker. His employer, McDonnell Douglas, sent him as an industrial payload specialist, at company expense, to the International Space Station in 1984 and 1985. Others have also flown, including a Japanese journalist and a British chemist, both of whom visited the Soviets' Mir space station in 1990.

The first civilian NASA chose to fully train as an astronaut and send into space, in the space shuttle *Challenger*, was teacher Christa McAuliffe in 1986. Congressman Bill Nelson flew on the space shuttle *Columbia* sixteen days before the *Challenger* launched. He later became the administrator of NASA.

But how does someone who isn't a politician, a government contractor, or a trained astronaut get to space? They pay for it. And it costs a lot!

Billionaires in Space

The first person to pay his *own way* to space was Dennis Tito, a billionaire businessman. Tito first approached NASA with the idea, but the agency refused to ferry anyone who was not a professional astronaut. Tito then turned to the Russians. In 2001, he gave Roscosmos $20 million to hitch a ride on a Soyuz rocket with two cosmonauts who were commuting to the ISS. What did Tito do there? He spent a week watching pencils float around the Russian module and videotaping Earth through its portholes. Over the next twenty years, several other civilians journeyed to the ISS on Soyuz, for the same price.

A couple of other American billionaires went a different route and decided to build their own rockets to launch themselves into space—or at least into the vicinity of space. In July 2021, after nearly two decades of hard work, inventiveness, and experimentation, their space vehicles were finally ready.

Both Richard Branson, founder of Virgin Galactic, and Jeff Bezos, founder of Blue Origin, boosted themselves—and a few passengers—about 50 miles above Earth. Their space vehicles soared into suborbital space, just high enough to experience weightlessness for about three or four minutes. The success of these two launches spawned even more trips for civilians to space.

One Round-Trip Ticket to Space, Please

What if you don't know a billionaire well enough to hitch a free ride but you want to float around in near space for a few minutes? You buy a ticket—for a lot of money. In 2023, Virgin Galactic advertised a ninety-minute ride for $450,000. Blue Origin does not release the cost of its flights to the general public, but they are said to be quite pricey as well.

What might space tourism look like? Just as there are many ways to take a trip on Earth, the same could be true for out-of-this-world vacationers. Want a pared-down jaunt? Opt for a few minutes of suborbital weightlessness. That could be a ride in a pressurized crew capsule. Or you might like a trip in a special high-altitude renewable-hydrogen balloon. (Don't worry, there is more than just a wicker basket on this balloon.) Prefer a "luxury cruise"? Go for three days in orbit around Earth. There's even talk of orbiting or landing on the Moon. But that's in the far-off future, if ever.

It Helps to Have Rich Friends

Branson and Bezos hosted a mix of friends, family, and paying customers. Branson invited Virgin Galactic employees with him on SpaceShipTwo. A couple of them had already run test flights of the winged rocket plane to be sure the seats and suits were comfortable.

He also brought the youngest person and the oldest person at the time to have ever ventured into the realm of space—a Dutch teenage whose $28 million fare was paid for him, and eighty-two year-old Wally Funk.

In 1961, Funk was one of the "Mercury 13." This was a group of women who were tested unofficially by the person at NASA in charge of developing rigorous physical, neurological, and psychological exams for astronauts-to-be. Funk easily handled six G's (a measure of acceleration) and more than ten hours in the isolation chamber—longer than anyone else. But NASA had no program for female astronauts.

She applied to be an astronaut three more times but was not accepted because she lacked an engineering degree. That did not stop Branson from inviting her for what she described as "the chance to make my dream a reality."

Crew Capsule, Spaceplane, or Balloon?

BLUE ORIGIN *NEW SHEPARD* CREW CAPSULE

Seats up to six people—a Blue Origin engineer and five passengers. It is designed to ascend to 62 miles (100 km), reaching speeds of up to 2,000 mph. The best part of the ride? The few minutes of weightlessness while enjoying stunning views of the planet below.

VIRGIN GALACTIC VSS *UNITY* SPACESHIP

Seats up to six people—two pilots and four mission specialists (who could be tourists). The spaceship is attached to its "mothership," VMS *Eve*, a large airplane that does not go into space. Instead, the mothership carries the spaceship to an altitude of about 45,000 feet, then releases it. From there, the VSS *Unity*'s rocket boosting motor engages, propelling it to higher than 264,000 feet (50 miles, 80 km), just at the edge of space. The crew experiences weightlessness and the view of a lifetime of the Earth below.

SPACE PERSPECTIVE'S BALLOON *SPACESHIP NEPTUNE*

A company called Space Perspective is developing *Spaceship Neptune,* a giant SpaceBalloon™ carrying a pressurized crew capsule that ascends to the edge of space (about 100,000 feet or 20 miles above the Earth's atmosphere). Accommodating eight Explorers and a Captain, a journey aboard *Spaceship Neptune* lasts six hours. Designed to be the safest, most accessible, and comfortable way to travel to space, Space Perspective's carbon-neutral spaceflights offer panoramic views through the largest windows ever flown to space, Wi-Fi, a world-class culinary program, and even a bathroom (the Space Spa) for the price of $125,000 per seat.

ZERO G EXPERIENCE

Don't have a lot of money but want to experience weightlessness? Take a trip on a Boeing 727 as it executes multiple parabolic maneuvers, the way the Inspiration4 team did. The plane takes off and climbs to 24,000 feet. The specially trained pilots then push the plane at a 45-degree angle to 32,000 feet and dive down. Passengers experience weightlessness for about ten to fifteen seconds. Each trip guarantees up to fifteen parabolas. The open area allows passengers to float freely and safely. The price is much more affordable, at just under $10,000.

SIERRA SPACE'S DREAM CHASER

While the other vehicles in this list take passengers on a ride to the edge of space, Sierra Space's Dream Chaser aims to go farther. This spaceplane is being designed to take cargo to the ISS. Like the space shuttle, it is launched on a rocket, but it can also land like a plane. And Dream Chaser is equipped with ceramic tiles, similar to the ones used on the space shuttle, which enables it to survive the searing heat as it travels through Earth's atmosphere.

The vehicle will be operated remotely. It is not built to carry humans, but that possibility is not ruled out since the cabin inside will be pressurized to allow astronauts on the ISS to remove and add cargo for the return trip. Will spaceplanes like this be the "thing" of the future? It's certainly exciting to think so!

The ISS has also played host to private groups. In 2021, a Russian film crew turned part of the ISS into a movie set. Actors included the film's stars, who flew up there on a Soyuz craft, as well as actual on-orbit cosmonauts. The filming went on for twelve days. The same year, a group of civilians traveled to the ISS in a SpaceX Dragon spacecraft. The tourists, however, got more than they'd bargained for. They had only planned to spend eight days on the ISS but ended up staying for fifteen. Why? The same reason a lot of airline flights are canceled: bad weather at their landing site in Florida.

NASA has also jumped into the space tourism industry. Its first private astronaut mission with Axiom launched four people on a SpaceX Falcon 9 rocket in 2022. As many as two more trips per year are planned. Axiom doesn't share cost information but NASA has said the company charges each customer about $55 million, depending on the length of the trip.

It's not just Americans and Russians who are opening space travel agencies. China plans to start offering trips to its Tiangong space station. So does the Indian Space Research Organization (ISRO), which announced a price of $700,000 per seat beginning in 2030.

Thinking of Going?

Both astronauts and private citizens exclaim about the chance to see Earth from a different perspective. Many comment on the "overview effect"—seeing the curvature of our planet from afar. Some say they have a feeling of being so small in the universe. Sian Proctor, one of the passengers on Inspiration4, savored the glow of "Earth light." Many people notice that there are no borders between countries.

Floating in microgravity is also high on tourists' lists. Decidedly fun. But beware: many people experience space sickness—yes, even astronauts! It feels like seasickness on a rocking boat or motion sickness on a fast roller coaster.

Are Spaceplanes the Same Things as Airplanes? No.

The NASA space shuttle was the first "spaceplane." A spaceplane must be able to operate like a spacecraft in space, re-enter Earth's atmosphere, and land like a plane.

The US Air Force owns American spaceplanes, officially called X-37B Orbital Test Vehicles. The capabilities of the X-37B are still being tested and are kept very secret.

We know that the spaceplane is small—less than thirty feet in length—and unmanned, and it needs to be boosted to reach space. In December 2023, two X-37Bs got a boost from a SpaceX Falcon Heavy.

China also has a spaceplane, but little information is available about it. Both countries' spaceplanes were unmanned as of June 2024.

Am I an Astronaut or a Tourist?

If you go to space, are you an astronaut? While that might sound like an easy question to answer, these days it's not. Derived from the Greek words meaning "space sailor," "astronaut" could refer to anyone who flies in space. But according to NASA, astronauts are people who "have been launched as crew members aboard NASA spacecraft bound for orbit and beyond."

To become a NASA astronaut a person must meet the following minimum criteria:

- Be a US citizen.
- Possess a master's degree from an accredited institution in a STEM field, including engineering, biological science, physical science, computer science, or mathematics.
- Have at least two years of related professional experience after degree completion, or at least a thousand hours of pilot-in-command time on jet aircraft.
- Pass the NASA long-duration flight astronaut physical.

The call for new astronaut classes opens only rarely, and selection is extremely competitive. NASA may accept only seven to ten applicants. Then it can

Where Does the Money Go?

Fares to space vary depending on the type of excursion. If you decide to hang out on the International Space Station for a while, you have to cover NASA's costs, which include (in 2023 prices):

- $2,000 per day for food
- $20,000 per km for trash disposal
- $130,000 per hour for ISS crew time on orbit
- $5.2 million per mission for ISS crew time for logistics support

take two years or longer to complete the astronaut training. In the end, there is no guarantee that a person trained as an astronaut will go to space. A precious few have had that honor.

What are civilians who go into space called? Are they astronauts, too? The answer is complicated. NASA refers to people who go to space on commercial vehicles, but are not trained by them, as "private astronauts." The Federal Aviation Administration calls them "spaceflight participants." If they are trained and meet other requirements, they can conduct activities that support NASA.

Are the members of Inspiration4 considered astronauts? Perhaps not by NASA, but the FAA says they are eligible for astronaut wings. To receive this honorary award, a person must

- meet specific requirements for flight crew qualifications and training, including the ability to withstand high acceleration and deceleration, microgravity, and vibration;
- demonstrate flight beyond 50 miles above the surface of the Earth as flight crew on an officially licensed launch or reentry vehicle; and
- demonstrate activities during flight that were essential to public safety or contributed to human spaceflight safety.

By this definition, the Inspiration4 crew are eligible to receive astronaut wings from the FAA, a US government agency. Are the individuals who experienced a few minutes of weightlessness below LEO on Virgin Galactic and Blue Origin spaceships also eligible for this award? The response might depend on whom you ask. They certainly did not undergo the rigorous training that Isaacman required of his crew. Nor did they meet the other FAA criteria. Still, Richard Branson says they are.

It Could Matter Whether or Not You're an "Astronaut"!

Article V of the Outer Space Treaty says that in case of "accident, distress, or emergency landing . . . astronauts . . . shall be safely and promptly returned." Who, exactly, are those "astronauts"?

Does the term refer just to the people whose governments have sent them on a mission? Or does it also include, say, SpaceX employees who travel to the ISS to deliver equipment? Or is it every thrill-seeker who reaches suborbital flight?

The Rescue Agreement, which the UN adopted very shortly after the Outer Space Treaty went into force, broadens the category of who needs to be rescued by referring to "personnel of a spacecraft." The term "astronaut" is not defined. Therefore, it is unclear whether it only refers to astronauts who go into orbit or also those who are in suborbital flight.

Lawyers love to argue about issues like this. And they will be arguing the instant the first private citizen goes astray in space—or near space. But we are obligated to help each other.

What If the Worst Happens?

As with many types of exploration, there is a risk of great danger. NASA and all the other space agencies do everything they can to keep astronauts safe. Still, the unimaginable happens.

On January 27, 1967, the Apollo 1 command module was sitting on the launch pad. Astronauts Virgil "Gus" Grissom, Ed White, and Roger Chaffee were conducting tests inside. After a difficult day with many delays, the worst thing that could happen did: fire! A spark ignited in the module, which was filled with pure oxygen, causing the fire to accelerate rapidly. The astronauts were unable to open the hatch to escape, and the engineers on the outside couldn't help. The three astronauts perished. After this horrible tragedy, NASA took the time to re-evaluate every process, every material, every system.

Almost twenty years later, another tragic event occurred. The space shuttle *Challenger*, carrying seven crew members—including teacher Christa McAuliffe, exploded and broke apart less than two minutes after it launched. All of the crew were killed. This accident set the Space Shuttle Program back several years. The program was grounded until NASA discovered the cause.

Improvements were made and the program was restarted in 1988, after a hiatus of two years and eight months.

Things went well until February 1, 2003, when the space shuttle *Columbia* broke up on reentry. A large piece of foam had fallen off during launch and damaged the heat shields on the shuttle's wing. The exposed area, without heat shields, allowed the extreme heat during reentry to enter the shuttle. All seven crew members were lost.

Space travel is not without its dangers. Anyone who is thinking about going into space needs to be aware of them.

How Risky Is Space Travel?

Back in the early 1980s, when the first space shuttles were lifting off, NASA figured the chance that a flight could end disastrously was one in nine. That's a scary number! But the engineers learned a lot from the *Challenger* and other disasters. And they've been building extra safety features into every craft, and extensive system checks into every flight.

Risk Numbers

Calculating the risk of an activity is complicated. But the final numbers aren't hard to understand.

A one-in-nine chance that an accident might happen means that, over time, about one-ninth of all the trips might not end well. It doesn't mean that there will be an accident the ninth time a flight takes off! If it did, no one would get on it. So a chance that one in three hundred trips might have trouble is much less risky than one in nine.

So, by the time Inspiration4 took off, NASA calculated the chance of a failure at about one in three hundred.

Companies that fly private citizens to space must tell them everything that could go wrong. Then the passengers sign a form, called "informed consent," stating that they understand the dangers. They also promise not to sue the company, no matter what happens. Many citizen astronauts, including those on Inspiration4, write a letter to their family before launch, just in case they don't return. Proctor composed a poem, in which she said, "It's all I've ever wanted."

Rules? What Are Those?

Seeing how hazardous it is, you might think that spacefaring companies that take tourists for rides to or near space would be required to follow some safety procedures. After all, products ranging from hair dryers to rollercoasters can't be sold until they're inspected and declared safe for public use. So making sure space tourists' helmets are airtight would make sense, right?

Nope. In 2004, the United States Congress decided to *stop* regulating—putting such requirements on—the commercial space industry. *Why did they do that?*

The short answer is: the X Prize.

In 1996, an entrepreneur named Peter Diamandis announced a prize to promote space travel for the general public. He hoped to inspire space entrepreneurs just as a prize, which had kicked off the barnstorming era over a century ago, had inspired the aviator, Charles Lindbergh. Diamandis and the Ansari Foundation would award a $10 million prize for the first privately built craft to reach space. There were just a few contest rules. The ship had to be able to carry at least three people, reach an altitude of at least 100 km (62 miles), and do it all over again within two weeks.

Twenty-six teams from seven countries

Barnstorming Space

Miss Lillian Boyer demonstrates aerial acrobatics in 1922.

During the 1920s, daring airplane pilots called barnstormers put on stunt shows around the country, performing loops and swoops and even dancing on the wings. These flying circuses were hugely popular. Not surprisingly, though, there were accidents. By the end of the decade, Congress stepped in and adopted safety rules that pretty much shut down the whole business.

No one is suggesting performing wild stunts in space. But many people want the industry to have its own "barnstorming era."

vied to meet the deadline of January 1, 2005. On September 29, 2004, a rocket-powered vehicle called *SpaceShipOne* roared off from the Mojave Air and Space Port test center. It reached 100 km above the desert and glided back down twenty-four minutes later. Astronauts and cosmonauts on board the ISS congratulated the pilot for joining them, briefly, in space. After repeating the feat five days later, the design team walked off with the $10 million prize. (The winning company soon morphed into Virgin Galactic.)

This first successful, privately funded journey into space was tremendously exciting. People predicted ten thousand flights within a decade! Tourists galore! Inflatable hotels! To encourage these innovations, American executives lobbied their senators and representatives to stay out of their business. Rules cost time and money. Leave us alone!

Congress listened and, in 2004, passed the Commercial Space Launch Amendments Act. This law banned any regulations that might protect the health and safety of crew or passengers on private spaceflights. Then they amended *that* law in 2015 to make it absolutely clear that spaceflight participants cannot sue a company that injures them or sets them adrift in space.

The idea is that too many rules can end up grounding spacefaring companies before they take off. No one knows yet whether it's better to ride a rocket, a balloon, or a plane—or something else—to space. Meanwhile, a free-for-all atmosphere might be the best way to encourage innovation—until there's an accident, that is.

Are changes to commercial space regulations looming? Perhaps. The Commercial Space Launch Amendments Act was set to expire in late 2024. Some organizations are pushing for safety regulations and for ways to rescue space passengers, if need be. It will be interesting to watch what happens with this. Adding regulations typically means adding a lot of costs. How will the commercial space companies feel about that? Will they be increasing the price for passengers? It's a possibility.

As of mid-2024, US space companies that carry tourists had to follow only two requirements: get a license from the Federal Aviation Administration and promise to protect people on the ground. In fact, the informed-consent form that the Inspiration4 crew and other tourists signed reads in part: "The United States government has not certified the launch vehicle and any reentry vehicle as safe for carrying flight crew or spaceflight participants."

Space tourists, beware!

CHAPTER 10

Home Sweet Moon

THE ARTEMIS PROGRAM

Artemis I, the first integrated
flight test of NASA's deep
space exploration system
(artist's rendering).

We Are Going to the Moon!

The crowd was growing restless. Their eyes were trained on the gigantic orange and white rocket illuminated by spotlights. They practically willed it to lift off the pad. It was a typical Florida night in November at Kennedy Space Center—chilly and damp, and getting colder. However, this night was anything but typical. The gigantic Space Launch System (SLS) rocket was about to make its historic journey to the Moon.

Well, that's what everyone hoped.

Many people in the crowd had attended the two previous launch attempts. They knew that this launch was not guaranteed to happen either. But by 9 p.m. (EST) on November 15, 2022, everything was on schedule. Things were looking up.

Then another problem occurred. There was an issue filling the hydrogen tank on the Artemis rocket. Would this launch be scrubbed, too?

Not so fast. NASA called on its "red crew," a team of three men trained to go in and work on the rocket while it was on the pad. They bravely drove up to the fueled rocket and performed repairs to fix a leak.

The crowd cheered! It would launch!

Or, maybe not. One of the satellites designated to track the launch and provide important data to NASA was down. The rocket couldn't fly without it.

NASA Mission Control stopped the countdown clock with thirty minutes to go. They hoped that the clock could be restarted, but for that to happen, the satellite connection had to be reestablished.

WE ARE GOING!

Astronauts and astronaut candidates from NASA and the Canadian Space Agency pose for a photograph in front of NASA's Artemis I Space Launch System and the *Orion* capsule atop the mobile launcher on the pad at Launch Complex 39B at NASA's Kennedy Space Center in Florida, on August 28, 2022.

Everyone in the crowd held their breath and looked at their own watches. It was 1:04 a.m. The launch window was still open. NASA had two hours to launch the rocket or the mission would be scrubbed—again. Would they have to come back again on Saturday for another middle-of-the-night launch? Was all this time spent sitting on the cold, damp grass for nothing?

Suddenly, the call came. Charlie Blackwell-Thompson, the first female launch director at NASA, made the decision. . . .

Launch was a GO!

The countdown was quickly restarted.

Ten, nine, eight, seven, six, five, four, three, two, one . . . IGNITION!

With a huge blast of fire and an enormous white cloud of steam, Artemis I lifted off the pad. The flames from its engines were so bright they lit up the sky! It looked like daytime even though it was 1:47 a.m.

Artemis I ascended quickly. Since sound travels more slowly than the speed at which the rocket was moving, it took a few minutes for the blast of sound to hit the people on the ground.

Boom!

They heard the loud roaring and felt the rumble in their chests. But it was drowned out by the deafening cheers all around, the sheer joy and excitement of watching one of the most amazing pieces of technology and engineering come to life.

NASA had done it!

Artemis I was headed to the Moon!

NASA's Space Launch System rocket carrying the *Orion* spacecraft launches on the Artemis I flight test, November 16, 2022, from Launch Complex 39B at NASA's Kennedy Space Center in Florida.

This logo highlights the SLS rocket carrying the Orion spacecraft and lifting off from Launch Pad 39B at NASA's Kennedy Space Center. The orange rocket and flames represent the firepower of the SLS, and the three lightning towers represent the historic setting of Launch Pad 39B.

Artemis

In the Introduction, we addressed the question of why NASA is heading back to the Moon. Here is NASA's official answer:

> **We're going back to the Moon for scientific discovery, economic benefits, and inspiration for a new generation of explorers: the Artemis Generation. While maintaining American leadership in exploration, we will build a global alliance and explore deep space for the benefit of all.**
>
> **—NASA Artemis Program**

Between 1961 and 1972, NASA landed astronauts on the Moon six times. They explored the Moon's surface, drove a Moon buggy across it, and even brought back Moon rocks for study. These were remarkable accomplishments. And yet they were merely a beginning. NASA had always wanted more time on the Moon to study the lunar surface, to learn how humans could live there. With the Artemis program, NASA is heading back to the Moon . . . to stay.

The goals of the Artemis program are to

- prove that it is possible to send humans back to the Moon, to land and operate there;
- establish a permanent place to live on the Moon;
- establish a jumping-off point to other planets and perhaps beyond the solar system;
- allow for in-depth and in-person research about the Moon itself that will help humans better understand Earth and the other planets in the solar system; and
- create economic opportunity by expanding jobs and new technologies for a growing lunar workforce.

The Artemis program is an international partnership among NASA, JAXA (Japan Aerospace Exploration Agency), the CSA (Canadian Space Agency, and ESA (European Space Agency). Partners also include many commercial companies,

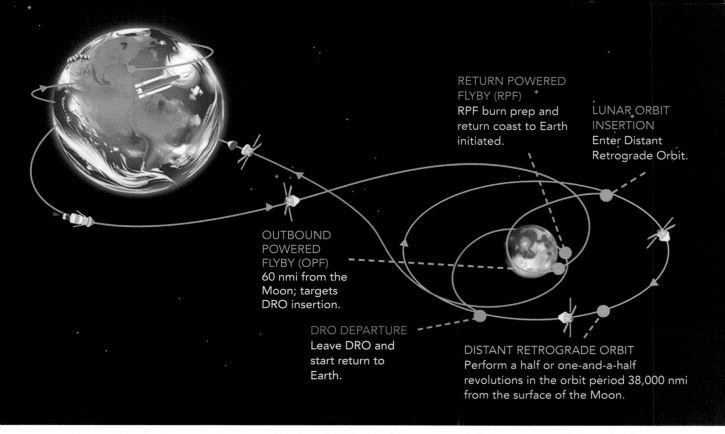

RETURN POWERED FLYBY (RPF)
RPF burn prep and return coast to Earth initiated.

LUNAR ORBIT INSERTION
Enter Distant Retrograde Orbit.

OUTBOUND POWERED FLYBY (OPF)
60 nmi from the Moon; targets DRO insertion.

DRO DEPARTURE
Leave DRO and start return to Earth.

DISTANT RETROGRADE ORBIT
Perform a half or one-and-a-half revolutions in the orbit period 38,000 nmi from the surface of the Moon.

Artemis I mission overview map. During this flight, the uncrewed Orion spacecraft launched on the Space Launch System rocket and traveled thousands of nautical miles (nmi) beyond the Moon over the course of about a three-week mission.

such as SpaceX, Lockheed Martin, Aerojet Rocketdyne, Boeing, Jacobs, Northrop Grumman, and others. All are dedicated to the idea of not only transporting humans to the Moon but also establishing a permanent place for research there.

Cislunar Space and the Moon

NASA and its international partners have spent the last two decades learning how humans can live and work in low Earth orbit. Living for weeks or months on the ISS is now routine. But LEO is not NASA's focus anymore.

NASA is turning its attention to cis-lunar space and beyond. That is what the Artemis program is about. The next step in human exploration of space begins on the Moon. To get to the Moon and beyond, a more powerful rocket is needed. The Space Launch System (SLS) is a massive rocket built to carry humans to the Moon, as well as supplies and equipment needed for them to live there. The Moon is quite far away from Earth and a rocket needs a huge push of energy to make it all the way, as we explained in Chapter 3 ("Where Is Space? Why Does It Matter?"). The SLS is just one of the rockets planned to get humans and supplies into cislunar space.

Building the SLS was a team effort led by NASA, three other space agencies, and over one thousand companies. Companies in every state in the US and in Europe contributed to this program.

Like the ISS, the Artemis program has taken years of research, trial and error, and the creation of brand-new technologies to make living on the Moon a reality. And there are still many new pieces of equipment and robotics yet to be created. What does some of this technology look like? Let's see.

Which Names Go with Which Parts of the Artemis Program?

A lot of terms are used to describe the rocket that NASA built for returning to the Moon. Should it be called Artemis? The Space Launch System (SLS)? The *Orion* spacecraft? They are all correct, depending on which part of the program you are referring to.

- Artemis is the name of the series of **missions** that will take humans to the Moon and eventually to Mars.
- The Space Launch System (SLS) is the **rocket** that has been designed to propel people and supplies through cislunar space and beyond.
- The *Orion* **spacecraft** will house the humans who will travel through cislunar space to the Moon and beyond.

Orion versus Apollo Spacecraft

The *Orion* spacecraft was modeled after the old *Apollo* spacecraft, but it has many upgrades.

The *Apollo* crew capsule did not have a bathroom. Instead, astronauts used bags to capture their waste. Food was freeze-dried and required water to be rehydrated. The *Apollo* crew capsule was quite small and did not allow much room for the astronauts to move about. Exercise was conducted in their seats by using a special resistance band to stretch and engage the muscles.

In the *Orion* spacecraft, the astronauts will have a bit more room. They will also have a bathroom! Other upgrades include a water dispenser to help astronauts stay hydrated, and a device to rehydrate and warm food. This makes food much tastier and allows for more variety. An exercise device enables astronauts to work out while in space, too. It can be used from the foldable crew seats. At night hammocks are strung up for the astronauts to sleep.

That's quite a lot of amenities to

Comparison of the *Orion* and *Apollo* capsules.

NASA is using new technology and lessons learned from earlier missions to build the new spacecraft. *Orion* will carry up to four astronauts compared with *Apollo*'s three, and a new version of the *Apollo* heat shield will keep the astronauts safe as the crew module re-enters Earth's atmosphere when it returns from deep space.

APOLLO

Crew module diameter: 128 ft.
Crew size: 3
Service module diameter: 13 ft.
Service module length: 24.5 ft.
Service module mass: 54,000 lbs.
Service module thrust: 20,500 lbs.
Power: batteries, fuel cells
Landing: water
Docking: lunar module
Destination: Skylab, Moon, Apollo-Soyuz Test Project

ORION

Crew module diameter: 16.5 ft.
Crew size: 4 (6 to ISS)
Service module diameter: 16.5 ft.
Service module length: 15.7 ft.
Service module mass: 27,500 lbs.
Service module thrust: 7,500 lbs.
Power: solar arrays, batteries
Landing: water
Docking: multipurpose
Destination: Mars, asteroids

Orion will use more modern technology in many other areas, such as computers, electronics, life support, and propulsion.

squeeze into a small spacecraft. But it's all necessary. Astronauts will live for days or weeks in the *Orion* module while they construct the Lunar Gateway, a space station that will orbit the Moon, which is discussed later in this chapter.

What Did *Orion* See?

The *Orion* spacecraft launched on Artemis I had sixteen cameras strategically placed on its exterior. The cameras captured information about the liftoff, deployment of the solar array, and piloting for the engineers at NASA's Johnson Space Center. But they also captured stunning views of the Moon for everyone on Earth.

These images did not disappoint. There are amazing close-up photos of the Moon as *Orion* passed just 80.8 miles (130 km) above the lunar surface. Craters, both deep and shallow, are scattered across the regolith. Photos like these have not been seen in over fifty years.

The Artemis I mission was a huge success! NASA proved that it could build a spacecraft and send it to the farthest position from our planet ever attempted (268,563 miles, or 434,523 km) and bring it safely back to splash down in Earth's ocean.

On flight day 13, *Orion* reached its maximum distance from Earth during the Artemis I mission when it was 268,563 miles away.

Space Launch System

The Space Launch System (SLS) is the most powerful rocket NASA has ever built. It's even bigger than the Saturn V, the rocket that propelled the last mission to the Moon. The core stage (main engine) of the SLS is a gigantic 212 feet tall and 27.6 feet in diameter. The Artemis I configuration, with the *Orion* spacecraft atop the SLS, stood 322 feet tall—taller than the Statue of

Two Rockets, One Destination

The two biggest rockets in the world—NASA's SLS and SpaceX's Starship—are going to take humans back to the Moon and beyond. How do they compare?

NASA's SLS is the tallest, heaviest, and most powerful rocket NASA has ever built. The SLS has been proven to work; it delivered the Artemis I spacecraft into space and sent it around the Moon. The SLS is designed to carry huge payloads to the Moon and eventually to Mars. NASA plans to continue with more Artemis missions using the SLS. A key point about the SLS is that it is not reusable. After launch, it falls into the ocean. NASA already has multiple SLS rockets in the pipeline, some of which have newly designed engines.

SpaceX's Starship, the most powerful rocket on the planet, proved that it could reach orbital velocity in March 2024. All signs indicate that it will continue to move toward its goal of reaching the Moon and beyond. Starship will produce more than 17 million tons of thrust (almost twice as much as the SLS). It will be able to carry 100 metric tons, or 220,000 pounds, of cargo to the Moon. Finally, Starship is supposed to be fully reusable. The rocket is designed to return to Earth after it has launched its spacecraft toward the Moon.

Both rockets are needed to support the future of human space exploration. In fact, NASA is counting on Starship to help build its Lunar Gateway space station. Using two spacecraft to transport pieces to build the Lunar Gateway is better than having just one.

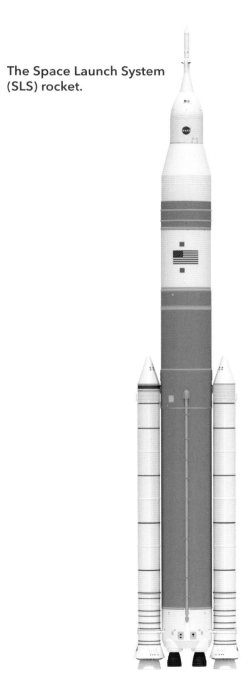

The Space Launch System (SLS) rocket.

Liberty. Not every Artemis mission will be of the same height.

The SLS has several different configurations, depending on what it needs to do. For Artemis I, with no crew and few supplies on board, the SLS weighed 5.75 million pounds and produced 8.8 million pounds of thrust during launch. That's 15 percent more thrust than was generated by the Saturn V.

What does this mean? It's a super powerful rocket and it needs to be! The SLS rocket will propel future Artemis missions that will carry astronauts around the Moon (Artemis II) and eventually allow them to land on the Moon. NASA envisions the SLS one day even propelling humans to Mars.

Artemis Missions II and III

NASA plans to send four astronauts around the Moon during the Artemis II mission. The four astronauts chosen for this historic mission will spend thousands of hours over several years preparing for their trip. They include: Jeremy Hansen (CSA), mission specialist; Victor Glover (NASA), pilot; Reid Wiseman (NASA), commander; Christina Koch (NASA), mission specialist.

As of April 2024, NASA is still planning for the Artemis III mission to land humans on the Moon again. The best-case scenario for launching Artemis III will be late 2026 or 2027. However, it is possible that Artemis III's mission might be altered to achieve a different goal. That would mean the Moon landing would occur on a future Artemis mission. The key to the Moon landing is that NASA must meet all of its required objectives for a successful mission: the new spacesuits must be ready to go, the *Orion* capsule must be refurbished and ready, and SpaceX's Starship must demonstrate its ability to launch successfully to the Moon.

It will also require that parts of the Lunar Gateway (or just "Gateway," described below) are in place, as well as the creation of a lunar lander, since *Orion* does not carry a lander with it.

Whichever Artemis mission goes back to the Moon, the result will be historic, seeing the first woman and the first person of color walking on the surface. As of early 2024, the mission is planning for the astronauts to be on the Moon for six and a half days, but that could change depending on the mission's timeline.

Six-and-a-half days would also be historic in terms of time spent on the

Astronauts chosen for the historic Artemis II mission from *left to right*: Jeremy Hansen, Victor Glover, Reid Wiseman, and Christina Koch.

Moon. It would be almost twice as long as Apollo astronauts remained on the Moon. But again, much of this is still in the early planning stages. Be sure to watch for more information. You won't want to miss this historic event!

Home Away From Home

Once the astronauts reach the Moon, they are going to need a place to stay. The *Orion* spacecraft is not designed to land on the Moon. It's intended only to orbit it.

So how will the astronauts get onto the Moon? The astronauts will transfer from Orion to the Lunar Gateway once docked there. From Gateway, they will have access to the Human Landing System (HLS), which will take them to the Moon.

The Lunar Gateway will be set up like a smaller version of the ISS. It will have a laboratory for conducting experiments, Mission Control for expeditions to the Moon, and a place to dock the HLS, which is designed to ferry the astronauts between the surface of the Moon and the Lunar Gateway.

Astronauts will be able to live and work on Gateway for up to three months. During that time, they will conduct experiments in its lab and make trips to the Moon's surface. Gateway is an international partnership among NASA, ESA, JAXA, and the CSA. Each partner country is contributing different equipment and modules.

An artist's rendering of the Gateway space station that will be placed into orbit around the Moon.

Robot House Sitter

Unlike the ISS, Gateway will not be continuously staffed. Not by humans, anyway. Canada has promised to deliver its Canadarm3 to Gateway.

This robotic arm will act autonomously, meaning that it can move on its own (according to how it's programmed). While astronauts are on Gateway, they can use the Canadarm3 to continue building it; repair it; move modules around, if needed; and even capture visiting vehicles for smooth docking . When the humans aren't on board, Canadarm3 will be able to still do all these things. It can also maintain itself, which means it can fix itself if it has an issue. It is the ultimate house sitter!

The Canadarm3 will be installed on Gateway and will perform many tasks, including capturing visiting vehicles, assisting astronauts with spacewalks, and helping with maintenance and repair of the space station.

The Lunar Space Laboratory

Gateway will provide unprecedented opportunities for exploration of space. Within its titanium walls, scientists hope to uncover the answers to some big questions about space. Can humans live and work in deep space for long periods of time? Will the human body survive the exposure to intense solar radiation and solar winds on and near the Moon? The Earth has a magnetosphere, a region surrounding our planet in which Earth's magnetic field dominates and protects our atmosphere from solar particles and energy that stream toward us. The Moon does not have a magnetosphere and so cannot provide this protection for astronauts.

While orbiting the Moon, Gateway

The design for Artemis III's human landing system began back in 1969, when NASA examined several ideas for landing the Apollo 11 astronauts on the Moon. The most direct approach would have sent a rocket straight from Earth to the Moon. But the rocket would have had to be huge, and landing it nose-up and tail-down on the Moon so it could take off for the return trip would have been extremely tricky. A slightly more realistic idea involved assembling rocket parts in Earth's orbit. But again, lunar liftoff was a challenge.

The winning suggestion—to assemble a landing system in lunar orbit—was ridiculed and then ignored for months, until a persistent engineer named John Houbolt skipped over the chain of command and wrote a letter directly to a top administrator. Calling himself "a voice in the wilderness," Houbolt explained the weight and cost savings and convinced NASA of this elegant solution, which would be reconfigured and used again sixty years later.

will be nearer to the Sun, making a more detailed study of it possible. Perhaps scientists will learn the causes of solar flares and the origins of dust on the Moon.

Constructing Gateway in space will require multiple trips from Earth; it's too big to launch as one piece. Each piece will travel up as a single module. Then the pieces will be attached to each other in space, using Canadarm3.

The initial two sections of Gateway are planned to launch on a SpaceX Falcon Heavy rocket. These are the power and propulsion element (PPE) and the habitation and logistics outpost (HALO). Some of the additional sections and equipment for Gateway will travel on SLS rockets via Artemis missions. Sometimes the rockets are larger to accommodate more payload (or parts of Gateway).

Human Landing System

NASA has offered a contract to SpaceX to create one of the human landing systems, or HLS. A different HLS will be created by Blue Origin. Each company will design its own device, based on guidelines from NASA. As a reminder, the HLS will serve as a "taxi" that will take the astronauts from Gateway to the surface of the Moon and back.

The HLS will also be the base for the astronauts while they are on the Moon. It will have enough space to house up to three astronauts for a few days, or even weeks, on the lunar surface. The HLS will have places to store samples and conduct small experiments and will be able to carry a lunar terrain vehicle (LTV) to the surface for wider exploration. (Think of the LTV as a space-age dune buggy of sorts, one that can bounce along—and in—the low craters of the lunar surface.)

Artemis Base

Eventually, NASA envisions that the astronauts will have a more permanent base on the Moon, big enough for up to four astronauts to live for a month at a time. The design includes a lunar cabin, a place to park the LTV, and a mobile home. Although it won't necessarily look like one on Earth, it will be home to the astronauts while they are on the Moon.

An artist's rendering of what a NASA base could look like at the lunar South Pole.

When you think of ice, you might think of a cube of frozen water, or perhaps the slick stuff on the roads in the winter. When ice melts it becomes drinkable water. The thing to understand is that the ice we know on Earth is not the type of ice you'll find on the Moon.

The Moon's water ice is in the form of tiny particles attached to bits of regolith, or Moon dust. For this water ice to be drinkable, it would have to be extracted from the regolith. That would most likely be difficult, but in the end, it might be easier to extract water from regolith than to transport it from Earth.

Why? Water is heavy. Heavier rockets need more energy. They also don't fly as far. People need water every day, so transporting enough water to keep astronauts alive in space, let alone on a base on the Moon, would be extremely expensive. Having useable water on the Moon would save on shipping costs.

This illustration highlights the Moon's Clavius crater and a depiction of water trapped in the lunar soil there.

How Will Humans Live on the Moon?

Building the base is just one part of living on the Moon. If humans want to make a home there, the base they build will need to be self-sustaining. This would eliminate the constant need for supplies from Earth just to survive. Since the Moon is so far away, sending supplies there on a regular basis would be difficult and very expensive.

That is why NASA, along with many commercial companies, is investigating ways to use the resources on the Moon to create a habitable environment.

NASA is targeting the South Pole of the Moon as a place to build its first Artemis base camp. That is because the craters at the South Pole have areas around their rims where the sun shines continuously. By harnessing solar energy, the base camp would have a continuous source of power.

The bottoms of the craters are very dark and get little to no sunlight. There, NASA believes, it might find water ice. Water is one of the most precious resources required in space.

Without water, humans cannot survive. Of course, they can't live very long without oxygen either.

Scientists believe that water molecules are either embedded in the regolith beneath the surface and/or found as particles sticking to the Moon dust. Turning those molecules into useable water is not going to be easy. But if water exists on the Moon in some form, you can be sure that scientists and engineers will be investigating ways to use its two components. Hydrogen for fuel. Oxygen for breathing.

Finally, the astronauts probably would like to eat something other than food in tubes. Not only does that get tiresome, but it's also not healthy over the long term. Will humans be able to grow food on the Moon? Maybe. They will have to construct special greenhouses where temperature and pressure are strictly controlled. But scientists believe it can be done. After all, the tiny greenhouses on the ISS are full of fruits and vegetables that have been grown—and eaten—in space.

Would You Like to Live on the Moon?

Some day, far in the future, it might be possible for you to visit the Moon. Perhaps even live on it. Between now and

Spiffy New Space Suits, Too!

Astronauts on the Moon will need special suits, too. These suits must be able to protect them from the high radiation and solar flares that they could encounter on the lunar surface. And let's not forget the dust. Tons of dust containing bits of regolith cover the surface. All that dust gets onto the astronauts' suits—but not inside, of course. Astronauts will be kept cool or warm in the suits. The space suits will be flexible enough to allow astronauts to bend and move, but also airtight to prevent any oxygen from escaping—or worse, the pressure from dropping. Like all clothing, the suits are designed to be comfortable, safe, and cool looking, too.

Kristine Davis, a spacesuit engineer, is wearing the prototype of NASA's new spacesuit, the Exploration Extravehicular Mobility Unit (xEMU).

then huge amounts of technology will need to be developed, which requires solving lots of problems. How do we extract water from regolith? How would people who travel to different regions of the Moon tell time? (ESA and NASA are already working to establish a lunar time zone.) What might you do on the Moon? At some point in the future, will the Internet be available, so you could attend school up there while looking out your window at the Earth?

The quest to live on the Moon is just beginning. Space agencies and commercial companies are hard at work building pieces of the Gateway, the Human Landing System, and the Artemis base that will make the Moon habitable for humans. It will be up to your generation to lead the way.

While the timetable for Artemis missions may slip by months or even years, the additional time needed will be well spent. After all, the engineering and design of the equipment must be accurate, precise, and, above all, safe for humans.

In the next chapter you'll learn how commercial companies around the world are working to establish a presence in cislunar space.

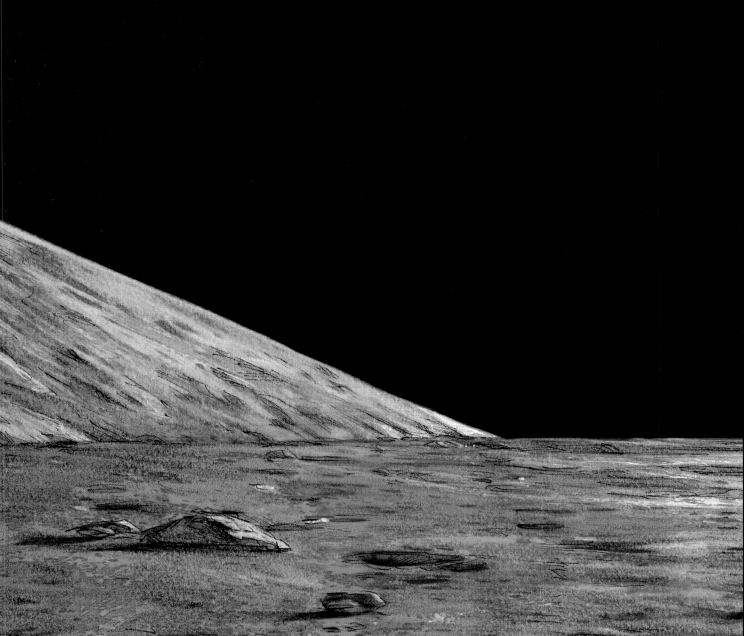

CHAPTER 11

Howdy, Partners!

DOING BUSINESS IN SPACE

Catching a Ride with SpaceX

In March 2020, the world was shutting its doors. The COVID-19 pandemic pushed billions of people into isolation. Schools closed. Businesses sent their workers home. Travel practically came to a halt.

But NASA needed to keep flying.

In May 2020, astronauts Doug Hurley and Bob Behnken were scheduled to lift off for the International Space Station. This undertaking was critical. NASA workers monitored the spread of the pandemic, donned masks, and kept showing up at the office.

Employees at SpaceX did, too. Why? Because they were responsible for ferrying Hurley and Behnken to the ISS. This was a departure for NASA, which had been using a Russian Soyuz spacecraft for the past nine years. Now the astronauts were to travel on a Falcon 9 rocket and Crew Dragon spacecraft, vehicles designed and built by SpaceX.

And neither NASA nor SpaceX personnel on the ground nor the astronauts would control the vehicle during most of the flight. Unless Hurley and Behnken ran into trouble, every operation would be handled autonomously by the Crew Dragon's software. This would be a mostly hands-off flight for these veteran pilot-astronauts.

Despite the pandemic and other setbacks, SpaceX's Falcon 9 rocket launched from the Kennedy Space Center on May 30, 2020. Company engineers in California oversaw the launch while NASA monitored the flight from the Kennedy Space Center.

The astronauts test-drove the controls a few times. They didn't use the typical array of manual controls. With their fingers they tapped three touchscreens, which looked like the interface for a video game.

"This is certainly different," Hurley had said during training. SpaceX design engineers had made sure the placement of the screens and arrangement of the displays suited the astronauts. Switching displays, they could see their location in space, monitor the pressure in the crew capsule or, if necessary, steer Crew Dragon.

SpaceX Crew Dragon spacecraft being prepared for testing in an acoustic test chamber, May 2018, before its first uncrewed flight in August 2018.

Astronaut Bob Behnken studies the Crew Dragon touchscreen before launching from Earth, and then docking with the ISS, May 2020.

Otherwise, the software was in control. As Crew Dragon slowly approached the ISS, the ring-shaped soft-capture mechanism maneuvered the craft to align precisely with the ISS's Harmony port entirely on its own. Click!

During their nineteen-hour ascent, Hurley and Behnken renamed their spacecraft *Endeavour*. This was a nod to history. Both men had previously flown on the space shuttle *Endeavour*, the last space shuttle to ever fly into orbit. Almost everything else about this flight, though, was a first:

- first transport of astronauts to the launch pad in a Tesla
- first NASA astronauts flown to the ISS on a private spacecraft
- first launch from US soil since the shutdown of the Space Shuttle program in 2011
- first recovery of a rocket booster on an autonomous drone ship, called *Of Course I Still Love You*
- first autonomous flight and docking at the ISS
- first splashdown in American waters since 1975

At the end of their two months on board the ISS, Mission Control greeted the returning astronauts: "Welcome back to planet Earth and thanks for flying SpaceX."

In this book, you've learned about several kinds of partnerships in space. Eighteen countries, including Russia, Canada, Japan, and the US, have teamed up on the International Space Station. Also, space agencies buy products and services from private corporations, such as the way NASA partnered with Northrop Grumman for the Cygnus spacecraft.

In this chapter, you'll read about two new types of partnerships:

- Commercial companies that are ferrying NASA astronauts to the ISS on rockets and spacecrafts that the companies design, build, finance, and own—and control.
- Companies that are planning to sell—but not deliver—lunar regolith to NASA.

Both of these arrangements are a departure from previous business models between NASA and commercial companies. They offer new opportunities for reaching space and obtaining resources on celestial bodies. These arrangements also entail technological and financial risks. And they raise conundrums.

Let's look at them one at a time.

Crew Dragon Is Cleared for Liftoff!

SpaceX's Crew Dragon ushered in a new path for NASA astronauts to fly to the ISS. It also pioneered a new way that NASA relates to businesses.

From the beginning of the Space Age in 1957 until 2020, government space agencies, like NASA, Roscosmos, ESA,and JAXA, were pretty much in charge of space. They decided who could go; they sent people up and brought them back down. They also gave the companies that built the spacecraft precise directions for how everything should look, work, and perform. And NASA engineers double-checked everything to be sure the companies were following those directions.

Things shifted dramatically, however, when Crew Dragon transported Hurley and Behnken to the ISS. Under the new arrangement called the Commercial Crew Program, NASA tells companies—Boeing and SpaceX as of 2024—only the purpose and goals of a launch. For example, three astronauts, their food, and any experiments must be sent to the ISS during a specific range of dates. That's pretty much it. No more detailed orders.

Then the companies can get creative, designing and building whatever system they think will do the job best. In the case of NASA's maiden voyage on Crew Dragon, SpaceX decided that its software would manage the flight better than the astronauts could. No more switches to flip and dials to turn!

The equipment must meet basic guidelines from NASA and pass rigorous safety tests, but NASA is no longer involved in the design and building of the rockets and spacecrafts. Once NASA approves the equipment, the agency contracts with the company to send its astronauts to space. NASA, in effect, buys round-trip tickets for the astronauts.

Why is this such a big deal? For one thing, the cost is much lower. Russia charged NASA as much as $80 million per astronaut to use the Soyuz rocket. Seats on SpaceX cost approximately $55 million to $58 million.

Also, since NASA won't have to fuss with managing the commute to LEO and back, it can become an "exploration agency." NASA can focus on deep-space Artemis missions to the Moon, and eventually to Mars, which we described in Chapter 10 ("Home Sweet Moon").

Companies Are Packing Up and Moving to LEO

With NASA looking toward the Moon and beyond, where does that leave commercial corporations? Their plan is to handle much of the traffic in LEO and, they hope, to make a large profit by doing so. Companies foresee one day ferrying robots to fix or remove broken satellites, or whisking a hundred tourists at a time into orbit and sending them on spacewalks. Some analysts think the total space economy—combining satellites, tourism, and every other aspect of the space biz—might be worth as much as a trillion dollars a year by 2030!

These ventures could be a win-win for both the public and private sectors. If many companies decide to send people to space, they will have to compete for passengers. Just like airlines on Earth, they may have to offer sales or lower prices to entice people to fill their seats to space. That competition could make space travel more affordable for the average person. Perhaps one day, many years down the road, there might be as many ways to get to LEO as there are to travel between Chicago and New York.

But if NASA is no longer focusing on LEO, will LEO be left to tourists and satellites? The answer is no.

NASA has another program, called Commercial LEO Development, that's working with two companies—Blue Origin and Nanoracks LLC—to design "free flyers." These will be *private* space stations. What will they do?

One section of a free flyer could be rented to NASA to conduct research in microgravity. Another section could provide space hotel rooms for tourists. Yet others could operate hydroponic greenhouses or refueling stations for satellite constellations. Free flyers could even serve as platforms for launching additional space stations.

No one knows for sure whether these ventures will be profitable. Certainly, the owners of these businesses will be taking financial risks. They could spend lots of money on ideas that sound great but never work. Or worse yet, that no one actually uses. Several space businesses have already gone bankrupt. Who knows how many more will do so?

Some folks at NASA are concerned that spacefaring companies will make money by beaming billboards down to earthlings. Would you like to see ads for sneakers blotting out your view of stars in the night sky? America has outlawed such "obtrusive space advertising." But other countries have not.

Does the Moon Have Rights?

An organization called the Australian Earth Law Alliance is concerned that people could alter the Moon, much as they've damaged Earth's climate. The members have issued a Declaration of the Rights of the Moon. It states, in part, that the Moon is "a sovereign natural entity." It has the right to "continue its vital cycles unaltered, unharmed and unpolluted by human beings."

Making sure that Moon Rights are honored would require international agreements, such as treaties. Countries would also need to limit what commercial companies are allowed to send aloft. Currently, such regulations do not exist.

That'll Be $5,000, Please—Or, Not

Let's turn to the second precedent that NASA and private companies are setting. This one involves companies that are planning to sell lunar regolith to NASA. The key point is that the companies are not actually delivering regolith to Earth. Instead, it stays right where it is, on the "feet" of a lunar lander on the Moon. It might sound odd, but NASA plans to pay companies for something it won't actually receive. The US government and the governments of other countries are passing laws allowing this to happen.

Not sure why NASA is doing this? Bear with us as we explain the situation. It's a big deal, and it definitely poses a conundrum.

$5,000 for Regolith That Stays Right Where It Is? What a Deal!

On April 25, 2023, dozens of staffers who worked for a Japanese company called ispace anxiously stared at their computer monitors. Why? They were awaiting the landing on the Moon of HAKUTO-R, a lander and robot that had started its journey from the Kennedy Space Center four and a half months earlier. If all went well, their craft would not only be the first *commercial* lander on the Moon but also ispace could sell the regolith sticking to its pads to NASA. HAKUTO-R just needed to send a photograph to confirm its presence on the Moon. Estimated time of arrival: 12:40 p.m. (EST)

At 12:30 p.m., the lander reappeared from the far side of the Moon. This was a huge accomplishment for ispace engineers, but they weren't ready to celebrate yet. They knew that in five minutes, they would lose all communications with HAKUTO-R and would not know its fate until it signaled its safe arrival. During the final moments, an announcer displayed visual simulations and described the lander's expected path.

12:37 p.m. At 7 km above the Moon, the lander would slow to 700 kph.

12:39 p.m. At about 1 km above the surface, HAKUTO-R would rotate itself into a vertical, pads-first position. At 700 meters, it would slow to 100 kph, then continue slowing as it approached its landing spot.

12:39:50 p.m. Several meters up, small thrusters would fire, allowing a controlled touchdown. Only ten seconds to go!

12:40 p.m. Silence. HAKUTO-R was supposed to reestablish contact with Earth. Was it in trouble, the team wondered?

12:45 p.m. Continued silence. The engineers feared something had gone badly wrong.

1:06 p.m. No communication from HAKUTO-R in over thirty minutes. The announcer reports, "We have to assume that we could not complete the landing on the lunar surface."

Although ispace's president, Takeshi Hakamada, was disappointed, the mission was still productive. The company's engineers had gathered significant data, allowing them to analyze what had happened and plan a fully successful mission next time. Also, a precedent had been set: at some point in the future—possibly soon—NASA would pay a company for the regolith it collects.

"We will keep going," Hakamada said. "Never quit the lunar quest."

A month later, an analysis revealed why HAKUTO-R was unsuccessful in achieving a soft landing on the Moon. In its last moments, onboard software mismeasured the vehicle's altitude, and it ran out of the fuel necessary to continue slowing its descent. Entering lunar gravity and controlling the speed are especially tricky. Both Israeli and Indian space companies had tried in the previous four years, but only space agencies had accomplished the feat.

Nevertheless, NASA still hopes to purchase regolith "in place," either from ispace, which plans to try again at the end of 2024, or from one of the other companies. Why on Earth—or on the Moon—would NASA pay $5,000 for Moon dust it can't get its hands on?

The answer is that it's not the regolith that's valuable. It's the transaction that is noteworthy. It establishes a precedent: private companies can legally buy and sell resources extracted from a celestial body. If a company collects lunar regolith and sells it to NASA, well, then the Moon is open for business.

Landing a spacecraft, or lunar lander, safely on the Moon is not easy. On Earth, atmosphere creates drag, a force that pulls on an object and slows it down. But the Moon with no atmosphere can't slow down the object's descent. Unmanned lunar landers like HAKUTO-R

The Google Lunar XPRIZE

Google helped jump-start the role of private businesses that wanted to enter the space domain on their own. In 2007, Google offered $20 million to the first privately financed team to land a rover on the Moon, make it roam 500 meters, and send back pictures and video of the feat. The contest's original deadline was 2014, but Google extended it to 2018 and upped the cash award. The contest expired without a winner, but ispace, an early entrant, kept working.

must use computers which fire thrusters to decrease the speed of the lander as it approaches the surface. Sometimes those thrusters work as planned, and sometimes they don't.

But on February 22, 2024, Intuitive Machines' lunar lander, Odysseus, managed a historic first. Odysseus became the first commercial lander ever to land successfully on the surface of the Moon. It was a terrific achievement!

While the equipment on Odysseus is gathering data, there is one small issue with the landing. It is tipped over on its side. How did this happen?

The Moon is extremely rocky and has many uneven areas on its surface. Onboard computers using artificial intelligence "steer" the landers to a preselected spot on the surface. There are tons of calculations for these computers to make. They must control the speed both horizontally and vertically. If the lander gets too low, it can hit the edge of a crater or a rock and cause the lander to move off course. This is what happened with Odysseus. Regardless of its unexpected position, this lander has secured its place in history. Hats off to the entire Intuitive Machines team! We hope that there will be even more successes from other commercial companies by the time this book is published.

From LEO to the Moon: What Happened to "The Province of All Mankind"?

You can't sell something you don't own. To sell regolith, a company would first have to claim ownership of it. Then, after paying for it, NASA would declare that the regolith belonged to the US government.

You might be wondering how Japan and the United States can own bits of the Moon. After all, as you read in Chapter 1 ("Flags on the Moon"), the Outer Space Treaty states that space and celestial bodies are

- "the province of all" humankind and
- "not subject to national appropriation."

So how can a private company in Japan sell moon dust to America? Does this mean that space and celestial bodies belong to whoever gets there first?

These countries agree that space itself doesn't belong to anybody. Neither do celestial bodies, just as the OST says. However, they are declaring that they can take possession of the stuff they remove from a celestial body. Actually, it's their legislatures that are making this claim.

The first one was the Japanese parliament, which passed the Basic Space Law in 2008. Among other things, this law encouraged private operators to acquire material on celestial bodies.

In 2015, the United States Congress passed the Commercial Space Launch Competitiveness Act. This law gives Americans the right to extract and own space resources on a first-come, first-served basis. Five years later, NASA signed contracts for "delivery in place" of regolith. Luxembourg and the United Arab Emirates soon passed similar laws.

So, through national legislation, a growing number of countries and private businesses are claiming the right to own whatever they can take from a celestial body. They can't own the Moon or asteroid or planet or comet itself or even the real estate on which they land or live. But they have agreed that they can own the resources they dig up. With contracts from NASA, businesses in the US, Japan, and Europe are already carrying out these laws.

Other countries disagree, strongly. Russia has complained that these laws contradict the Outer Space Treaty because they amount to a landgrab—or a Moongrab. The head of Roscosmos, Dmitry Rogozin, called it an "invasion." Indonesia said that poor countries could be left behind.

Mining the Moon: The Artemis Accords

Regolith is abundant on the Moon, and thanks to the laws passed by several countries, it's free for the taking—once you get there, that is. While regolith is not easy to work with since much of it consists of sharp, clingy shards, it could prove to be handy.

Engineers theorize it could be compacted into bricks to construct houses and store solar energy that could keep astronauts warm and their equipment humming. NASA is even testing the feasibility of using regolith to 3D print structures in space.

The real prize on the Moon, though, is what appears to lie beneath the surface, especially water ice, as we explained in Chapter 10 ("Home Sweet Moon"). The Artemis III astronauts will head to the best place to fetch it. And they probably won't be alone there for very long. Even though the Artemis missions have gotten a head start, private companies might

eventually join them. China, too, has a plan—called the International Lunar Research Station—to work with other countries and put down roots in pretty much the same location by 2030. And India not only landed its Chandrayaan-3 spacecraft there in 2023, it also retrieved information about the lunar surface—tremendous feats for the Indian Space Research Organization (ISRO)

It might seem that our Moon is spacious enough to host plenty of visitors without bumping into each other. However, the number of icy craters that are accessible—ones that aren't too steep and rocky for machines and people to descend—is very limited. Those requirements leave only about a dozen sites, totaling an area the size of five to ten Grand Canyons. Most of those are at the Moon's South Pole.

Multiple countries might decide to build bases there to take advantage of

7. Protecting Heritage: Outer space heritage is our shared heritage. Historic artifacts and sites will be protected and preserved.

8. Space Resources: Extracting resources (such as water or minerals) from the Moon, Mars, comets, and asteroids does not necessarily suggest that the terrain belongs to any country.

9. Deconfliction of Activities: Actions will be carried out with "due regard" for each other's safety.

10. Orbital Debris and Spacecraft Disposal: Countries commit to limiting the debris their actions might cause.

the same resources. It could start getting crowded, and disagreements might follow. To help keep relations friendly, more than three dozen countries have signed a document, called the Artemis Accords, laying out how they'll get along.

Here's a quick overview of its main points:

1. Peaceful Purposes: All activities on the Moon should be peaceful.

2. Transparency: Countries are to share how they plan to explore the Moon.

3. Interoperability: Everyone should be able to connect to each other's structures, machines, and communications systems.

4. Emergency Assistance: Aid is to be given to personnel in distress.

5. Registration of Space Objects: Objects launched into space are to be registered with the United Nations.

6. Release of Scientific Data: Countries will confer before they commit to sharing scientific information with the public.

There are a couple of wrinkles with the Artemis Accords. One is that, unlike treaties, they are not binding. That is, no one, not even any of the dozens of countries that signed them by mid-2024, is legally required to follow them. Still, they add meat to the bones of the Outer Space Treaty, which all spacefaring nations *have* signed. There is hope that countries that have not yet signed the Accords, such as China, will be good neighbors as well.

Another wrinkle is that the Artemis Accords applies only to countries, not to companies. Does that mean that private businesses can behave however they want on the Moon? Could they dig in secret or ignore safety zones? Possibly, although businesses based in nations that have signed the Accords are expected to follow them.

Some corporations have begun to sign on to a voluntary set of principles called the Washington Compact on Norms of Behavior for Commercial Space Operations. Those principles are somewhat similar to the Artemis Accords. Basically, whether companies or countries follow the Accords remains TBD—to be determined.

The Outer Space Treaty: State Responsibility

Space isn't a total free-for-all for private companies. The OST applies to them, too. Here's what the OST says about private activities in space.

Article VI
States . . . bear international responsibility for national activities in outer space . . . whether such activities are carried on by governmental agencies or by non-governmental entities. . . . The activities of non-governmental entities . . . require authorization and continuing supervision by the appropriate State.

Corporations know that the term "non-governmental entities" means them. This article of the OST says that these businesses can't head up to space until they get a go-ahead from their country's government. Also, their country will be watching them closely every centimeter

Deconfliction? What's That?

Article IX of the Outer Space Treaty says that countries should operate with "due regard" for each other. In Chapter 5 ("Spats and Mishaps"), we pointed out that people aren't sure what "due regard" means. The Artemis Accords provide an example: Countries should not interfere with or harm anyone else's activities on the Moon.

For instance, they should let others know exactly when and where they plan to dig for water ice. That's because moving regolith around could harm other countries' machinery in the vicinity. So, miners will set up short-term "safety zones" to warn others to stay away. The Accords require that these zones be temporary to make it clear that no one is attempting to claim ownership of the terrain. Sharing information and staying out of each other's way can reduce the chance that conflicts will arise—in other words, DEconfliction.

of the way. That's because, remember, the Liability Convention says that it's the country that has to pay for any accidents they cause.

The Outer Space Treaty: Forward and Backward Contamination

With the Artemis partners, China and its partners, and private enterprises possibly making plans to go to the Moon in the next decade, it could not only get crowded, the Moon could also be accidentally contaminated by microbes from Earth. In fact, it's possible that an Israeli company spread thousands of tardigrades when its Beresheet spacecraft attempted to land on the Moon in 2019. These microscopic "water bears" probably died, though, when the rocket crashed on impact. This problem is called forward contamination.

When astronauts, tourists, or miners return from the Moon, the opposite problem—bringing space-born microbes to Earth—could occur. This is backward contamination. NASA tried to protect Earth from any Moon organisms when the Apollo 11 astronauts returned in 1969, but later admitted there were some breaches. Fortunately, there are no microorganisms on the Moon.

In 1967, the writers of the OST foresaw the possibility of both kinds of contamination and made sure to try to prevent it. Here's what they wrote.

Where Do I Even *Begin* to Get Approval to Go to Space?

Some companies in the US complain about the American system for getting permission to launch spacecraft because it is complicated and time-consuming. Depending on what they want to do, business people might have to trek to three separate agencies:

- the Federal Aviation Administration (FAA) for approval for launch and reentry,
- the Federal Communications Commission (FCC) for radio frequencies, and
- the National Oceanic and Atmospheric Administration (NOAA) for remote-sensing satellites.

The paperwork alone can feel like it takes forever! As of 2023, the FCC had a backlog of 60,000 applications just for new satellites. To begin streamlining the process, the commission set up two new divisions: a Space Bureau, which deals with debris and other issues, and an Office of International Affairs.

Article IX

States . . . shall . . . pursue studies of . . . the moon and other celestial bodies . . . so as to avoid their harmful contamination and also adverse changes in the environment of the Earth resulting from the introduction of extraterrestrial matter.

Even though the OST doesn't spell out what "harmful" means, space agencies generally do everything they can to avoid the problem. It's not only a bad idea to spread foreign bodies around the cosmos, but also, doing so distorts scientific research. It might be hard to tell if a life form found on another celestial body was native or introduced by, say, a rover that was sent from Earth.

The United Nations directed a group called the Committee on Space Research (COSPAR) to set standards for "planetary protection." ("Planetary" here means not only planets but also moons and every other natural body floating in space.) One of the standards, for instance, requires that machinery be as sterile as possible.

COSPAR's job might be made especially complicated by companies that are heading to the Moon on their own. While space agencies and many space-bound businesses are fussy about cleanliness, some might be less careful. And no one is required to follow COSPAR's plan.

The problem of contamination and how to prevent it is definitely a conundrum to watch out for.

As you can see, there are likely to be a lot of opportunities for people to go to the Moon. Throughout the book, we've raised a number of conundrums about how they'll get along there and in space. Let's look at some options in the next chapter.

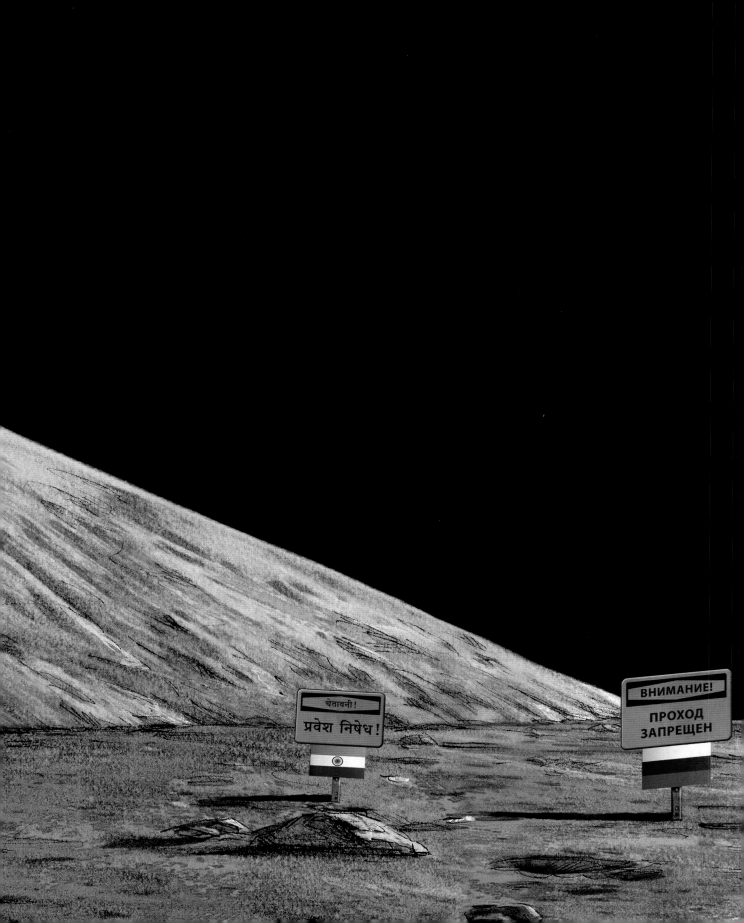

CHAPTER 12

Who's In Charge Around Here?

GOVERNANCE IN SPACE

> Policy can be even harder than rocket science!
>
> —Robin Dickey, Space Policy and Strategy Analyst, Aerospace Corporation

Conundrums

We've covered a lot of ground since you started reading this book. We have also asked some super-sized questions, like:

- How can disagreements in space be prevented?
- If disputes do happen, how will they be resolved?
- Will the first people to spend time on the Moon make the rules for everyone who follows?
- How can non-spacefaring nations share in the benefits of space exploration?

These conundrums are emerging because the technologies that are taking people to space and the Moon are evolving faster than the rules that are needed to govern them. It's like there is a space race between the engineers and the rule-makers, and the engineers are winning! This is actually on purpose. Scientists and engineers need room to use their imaginations. Too many regulations might limit their creativity.

The Outer Space Treaty says that space and celestial bodies are "the province of all" humankind, open to all. The upside is that no one controls them. The downside is that no one controls them.

No one wants space or the Moon to turn into a lawless Wild West. Yet there's no universal government that makes space laws. And don't hold your breath waiting for one. There are so many kinds of governments on Earth—democracies, monarchies, republics, autocracies—that people around the world aren't likely to agree on a central one for space.

So how can people govern themselves and each other to maintain peace and order there?

Let's do a quick recap of the ways we've mentioned that have worked so far. Then we'll look at some sticky situations people could get into in space and consider how they might get unstuck.

Governance in Space Since 1967

We've described several ways that spacefarers have kept themselves and each other in check.

Treaties

Treaties are useful because countries agree to agree with each other on issues they might not see eye to eye on. And, while hashing out the details, they make compromises, which they must then live with. That's because treaties are like laws: they must be obeyed, or else. (For more on the "or else," see below.)

The five major international treaties related to space are:

- **The Outer Space Treaty:** This is the granddaddy (and grandma!) of all space treaties. It says, in part, that no country can claim ownership of a celestial body. No weapons of mass destruction are allowed in space. International law applies everywhere. And space and celestial bodies are to be used only for peaceful purposes.
- **The Rescue Agreement:** All possible assistance should be given to astronauts in distress.
- **The Liability Convention:** Countries must pay for the damage their space objects cause on Earth and, when they're at fault, in space. This applies to objects launched not only by space agencies but also by private companies and anyone else.
- **The Registration Convention:** Countries must inform their own governments and the United Nations when they or a company based in their country sends something to space.
- **The Moon Agreement:** This one says that the Moon is "the common heritage" of humankind. That means countries must share what's on it. Very few countries have signed this agreement, so it's not really in force for most spacefaring nations.

Treaties can be hard to make, though. The more countries that are involved, the harder it gets.

National Laws, Regulations, and Directives

Another way to help ensure peace and safety in space is for individual countries to adopt laws requiring people to be good citizens. For instance, the US Commercial Space Launch Competitiveness Act, which we discussed in Chapter 11 ("Howdy, Partners!"), addresses managing debris in space.

Also, thanks to a US law, America and some other countries are supposed to let each other know about objects in space that might threaten them.

Rules, too, can be helpful. For instance, Canada, the US, and many other countries won't allow companies to launch satellites unless they show how they'll limit the debris they might cause over time.

Finally, countries can issue orders. For example, as of 2023, thirty-seven countries have joined the pledge to ban direct-ascent ASAT tests because they cause—you got it—lots of debris.

Norms

Leading by example can help set the right tone, too. When the International Space Station was established, the participating countries agreed to a chain of command for making decisions. Over the years, the astronauts onboard have developed ways of doing things that make sense. These actions have become standard and are therefore widely recognized "norms of responsible behavior." Everyone knows and accepts what to do and what not to do.

Sharing the science learned from exploring space, as China has done with their Moon rocks, is a great general practice. The countries that have signed the Artemis Accords hope that such actions become the normal way to do things.

Diplomacy

When tensions arise, simply talking can help. Just days after the Soviet Union launched the world's first rocket toward the Moon in 1959, Soviet Secretary Nikita Khrushchev and President Dwight Eisenhower turned down the heat by sitting down together.

The United Nations provides a setting where representatives from 193 countries can talk through their differences. The members have been doing so to keep space peaceful since 1967, and in 2023, UN Secretary-General António Guterres shared recommendations for governing outer space. The motto of the UN reads "Peace, dignity and equality on a healthy planet." Perhaps it should be expanded to include "and in space and on celestial bodies."

The International Telecommunication Union, (ITU) which we discussed in Chapter 6 ("Satellites and Where to Find Them"), is a quiet, hardworking agency within the UN that provides a good example of how to work things out. Radio waves and the telecommunications spectrum have one thing in common with water ice on the Moon: they are a limited natural resource in space. Sharing them *could* cause international tensions, possibly even conflict. This hasn't happened, though, because the ITU organizes the division and sharing of the signals. Every country in the world abides by its system practically all the time.

Sanctions

Countries can put sanctions on a country they find fault with. They might refuse to trade products or limit the number of tourists, for instance. After Russia invaded Ukraine, the European Space Agency sanctioned Russia by canceling a joint rover mission to Mars.

Generally, countries want to avoid penalties like these and will often change their behavior to ensure that the sanctions are removed.

Some Sticky Scenarios

How well will these methods work to prevent or reduce conflicts as more people spend more time off our planet? What other methods might be needed? When lawyers want to think through issues, they sometimes devise realistic but hypothetical cases. To help you ponder these questions, we've concocted some *unrealistic*, out-of-this-world situations.

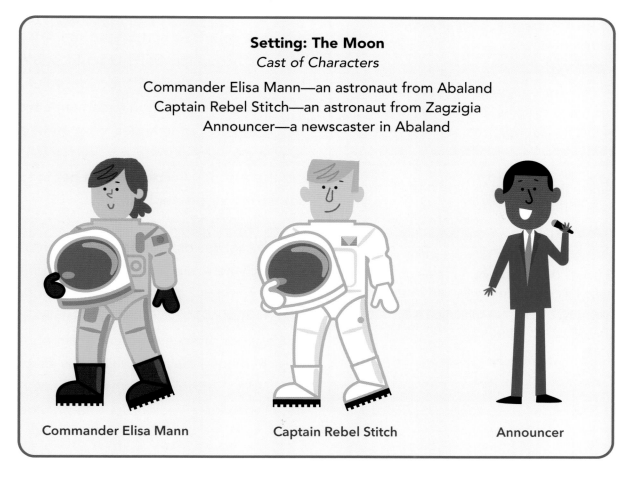

Setting: The Moon
Cast of Characters
Commander Elisa Mann—an astronaut from Abaland
Captain Rebel Stitch—an astronaut from Zagzigia
Announcer—a newscaster in Abaland

Commander Elisa Mann   Captain Rebel Stitch   Announcer

"That's My Spot!"
"No, It's Mine!"

It's eleven o'clock at night. But practically everyone in Abaland is awake and watching the news. That's because the first Abalandi, Commander Elisa Mann, touched down on the Moon a few hours ago! Here's the newscast from the capital city.

 Announcer: *"The hatch is opening. You can see the stairs descending. And there's Commander Mann, filming a selfie as she steps onto the regolith! Golly, this is exciting! But uh-oh. An astronaut is rushing over. And he looks irate. He's waving his arms and pointing. Commander, can you tell us what's happening?"*

 Mann: *"It's Captain Rebel Stitch from Zagzigia. He says I landed right in the middle of where he's digging for water, and he wants me to leave! He even built a fence around the area."*

Announcer: *"Is he allowed to do that?"*

Mann: *"Yes. The Artemis Accords say he can set up a safety zone, but it has to be temporary. Since no one else is here, he's been mining for three months. Anyway, no one has to obey the Accords since they're voluntary."*

Announcer: *"What are the two of you going to do?"*

If there were a Moon Government, the people who run it could help Commander Mann and Captain Stitch work out their differences. But there isn't.

The Outer Space Treaty says that no country can claim territory on the Moon. So the laws of Zagzigia and Abaland, whatever they might be, don't apply either.

Still, there are a couple of ways Mann and Stitch could find common ground. The fastest approach would be for them to talk and reach an agreement. They might look at the Antarctic Treaty and the UN Convention on the Law of the Sea. Both are shining examples of how countries can share open terrain.

If both countries had signed the Artemis Accords, then Stitch should abide by them, even though they are voluntary. That means he should dismantle his fence and let Commander Mann have a turn at the spot. Both talking and following the Artemis Accords would begin to set norms for proper behavior.

But what if Stitch refuses to move or what if Zagzigia did not sign the Accords? Here is where diplomacy and sanctions could come in. Abaland's ambassador could chat—quickly—with officials in Zagzigia or, if necessary, complain publicly. Perhaps Abaland, which has been supplying Zagzigians with their favorite jelly donuts, would refuse to provide them. Or the United Nations General Assembly might take a vote and condemn Stitch's behavior. Any of these actions *might* convince Stitch to move over.

"That's Mine!"
"No, It's Not!"
"Yes, It Is!"

Now that Stitch has moved aside and Commander Mann has had a chance to set up a small mining operation, let's check in with her.

 Announcer: *"Commander Mann, how are things going? Have you recovered any helium?"*

Mann: *"Oh, yes, lots. I was hoping to use it in the fusion reactor I'm building to create nuclear energy. But Captain Stitch says I can't do that."*

 Announcer: *"Why not?"*

Stitch: *"The reason she can't use the helium is that it's not hers. The Moon and everything on it belong to everybody on Earth—not just to Abalandis."*

 Mann: *"You were mining for water when I arrived!"*

Stitch: *"That was just for me to stay hydrated."*

Mann: *"Well, my government passed a law saying it's OK to remove helium. They sent me here to do that, and I intend to do my job."*

Abaland, where Commander Mann is from, is like the countries—the US, Japan, Luxembourg, and the United Arab Emirates—that have passed laws allowing their citizens to own regolith and other resources, such as helium. Zagzigians like Stitch, on the other hand, believe that the Moon's natural resources are like the Moon itself: they can't be owned by anyone. How can these two viewpoints be reconciled?

One possible resolution might be a treaty. Most of the treaties you've read about in this book involve multiple nations. Remarkably, 112 countries have signed the OST. But many treaties involve just two countries. Perhaps representatives from Abaland and Zagzigia could draft an agreement allowing Commander Mann to use a limited amount of helium. In exchange, she could share some with Captain Stitch or with other countries on Earth. It would be a good compromise, which is something that many treaties include.

The negotiations would not be easy or quick, because the issues are serious and complicated. A treaty between two countries would not solve the big question of who in the world, if anyone, owns Moon dust or helium. But the process of creating a treaty might allow the two astronauts to live and work side by side in peace.

"He Ruined My Reactor!"

 Announcer: *"It's wonderful, Commander Mann, that Abaland and Zagzigia were able to reach an agreement on helium. As a result, I understand that your reactor is up and running. Congratulations!"*

Mann: *"Well, it was all built, and I was about to turn it on when Stitch sabotaged the cooling system by hurling his wrench into it. That significantly damaged the reactor. So now it doesn't work."*

Stitch: *"She used more than the amount of helium our governments agreed on. If I hadn't stopped her, who knows how much she would have filched?"*

Neither of the astronauts is behaving well. Commander Mann violated their helium treaty. And Captain Stitch might have violated international law by damaging an object with his wrench. Both believe the other one did something wrong. But there's no judge on the Moon to decide who is right.

There are judges on Earth, though. The governments of Abaland and Zagzigia could bring cases against each other before the International Court of Justice (ICJ).

The ICJ, which is also called the World Court, was set up at the end of World War II in 1945. It is operated by the United Nations in a city called The Hague in the Netherlands. The court's fifteen judges, who come from all over the world, have two main jobs. They settle disagreements between nations, and they give advice, when asked, about issues of international law.

Sometimes, however, countries—especially the superpowers—don't accept the court's decisions, and they go unpunished. Also, governments must agree in advance to abide by the court's rulings. China, for instance, has not done so. When a fire-hot metal ring, very likely from a Chinese rocket, streaked down onto a village in India in 2022, the Indian government had no place to turn. The villagers had to figure out how to dispose of a 90-pound piece of a Long March rocket as well as a 60-pound metal sphere.

If Abaland and Zagzigia agree to abide by the ICJ's ruling, the judges could help the astronauts find a way out of their standoff. If either country refuses, they are out of luck. In particular, Commander Mann would be out one nuclear reactor.

"Snarl!" "Growl!"

 Mann: *"Yoo-hoo. Announcer, are you there?"*

 Announcer: *"Yes, Commander Mann. Do you need something?"*

 Mann: *"Yes. Weapons."*

 Announcer: *"Weapons? Why? I thought the International Court of Justice resolved your disagreement."*

 Mann: *"They did. Zagzigia had to pay to fix my reactor. But they haven't forked over the money yet. And I need to power my space station. I'm tired of waiting."*

 Stitch: *"Well, Abaland was supposed to pay a fine for her excess helium, but they haven't paid it yet either."*

 Mann and Stitch: *"This means war!"*

By this point, Commander Mann and Captain Stitch should be reminded of Article IV of the Outer Space Treaty: "Celestial bodies shall be used . . . exclusively for peaceful purposes." True, they don't sound very peaceful. Indeed they know that Article IV also forbids "nuclear weapons or any other kinds of weapons of mass destruction."

Long before they get anywhere near this level of hostility, Mann and Stitch could have turned to the Manual on International Law Applicable to Military Uses of Outer Space (MILAMOS) and to the Woomera Manual on the International Law of Military Space Operations. These documents compile the dozens of ways that countries agree on to avoid military activity on celestial bodies.

Reading through these documents might give them a broader perspective. In fact, Mann and Stitch might realize that they agree about more issues than they disagree about. Perhaps that would help them back off and lay down their arms—which, fortunately, they don't have (except for that wrench).

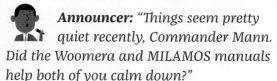

"Do I Really Have to Save Him?"

 Announcer: *"Things seem pretty quiet recently, Commander Mann. Did the Woomera and MILAMOS manuals help both of you calm down?"*

 Mann: *"It's definitely been calmer since Stitch disappeared."*

 Announcer: *"He disappeared?!"*

 Mann: *"He set off in his lunar rover for the far side of the Moon. I guess he wanted a vacation. Oh, wait. Here's a message from him."*

 Announcer: *"What does it say?"*

 Mann: *"He says, 'Help! My rover broke down. I'm afraid I'll run out of oxygen. Please, come get me.'"*

As you probably know—and as Commander Mann and Captain Stitch surely know—the Rescue Agreement directs her to find him and bring him back to safety. There might be circumstances that would excuse her from this duty. For instance, her rover might be low on fuel, or she might not have enough oxygen either.

But the preamble to the Rescue Agreement explains that it was created because of "the sentiments of humanity." That means that humans have an ethical obligation to reach out to each other in distress, even if it's hard.

We would like to think that Commander Mann will fetch Captain Stitch, that he will be grateful, and that they will support each other from now on. And also that Zagzigians and Abalandis will eat jelly donuts together on Earth.

Creating Space Amid Conundrums

We gave our sticky scenario a happy ending. That doesn't mean, though, that the conundrums we've raised are resolved. That's partly because many of them are just beginning to arise. While no one is mining on the Moon yet, it could happen in your future.

At each step, it seemed that Commander Mann and Captain Stitch found a way to come together. Nevertheless, their disagreements escalated. If they were real astronauts, the solutions they tried might work, at least for a while—or they might not. Sharing space on the Moon could get as sticky as regolith.

There's no way to know yet which of the methods for reaching decisions and keeping the peace in space and on the Moon will be successful. What's important is that there are many possible ways to do so. Spacefarers will need to try different options as problems present themselves in real life.

The Outer Space Treaty can be a springboard for solutions in a particularly important way. The OST presents a set of principles—beliefs and values about how to behave in space. You might have the chance to resolve conundrums using the methods we've discussed—or others you cleverly devise. If you do, think about the principles and priorities that *you* would most like people in space and on celestial bodies to live by. Promote the commercial development of space? Focus on research? Share the benefits of exploration with non-spacefaring nations?

We are leaving you with a lot of issues that don't yet have answers. We—and the world—are also handing you the opportunity to imagine the future you want in space. You get to go forth and create it. In the next chapter, you can find ways to take advantage of those opportunities.

CHAPTER 13

YOU Can Fly This Ship!

Thank you for joining us on this journey as we explored the technologies that are taking us back to the Moon and the laws and policies that are evolving to keep the peace. Within these pages you learned how the US went to the Moon for the first time in 1969, and heard from the very first International Space Station crew. You saw images of the Artemis program's planned return to the Moon, got a peek into the first commercial launch of the Crew Dragon, and tagged along with the Inspiration4 crew.

At the same time, you got a close-up view of the Outer Space Treaty and saw how it has served as the source of inspiration for later space treaties. Yet you also probably realized that the OST is not specific enough to resolve the conundrums that are arising as a result of new technologies. Policy needs to grow and change with the times. That is why governing bodies continue discussions to fill in the blanks. As our world moves toward inhabiting the Moon (and beyond), additional laws and norms will have to be created. Governments and commercial companies will need to work together to address situations that unfold as more people spend more time on the Moon.

While you've reached the end of this book, learning about the technology to get to the Moon and how to govern activity in space is just the beginning. This book has addressed a myriad of topics and technologies, though not all, of course. There are many more issues still to be solved, new technologies to be developed, and different places to explore.

It is our hope that you will take this book and use it as a jumping-off point for future discussions, as a way to familiarize yourself with new types of engineering and science and to learn more about policy and governance.

Where can you start? There are so many ways you can be involved in space! Too many to put into this book. So feel free to search the Internet and see what you come up with. It might surprise you. Here are a few career ideas to get you started.

The first one is obvious: you could be an astronaut. Becoming an astronaut is not easy. It takes many years of education and training. Still, astronauts get to be the first to explore new environments and celestial bodies.

Or if you don't want to travel in space yourself, you could work in a space-related field. There are many roles available here, and not just related to the Moon, but to every aspect of space.

Left, Megan McArthur participates in robotics proficiency training; *center,* Franklin Chang-Díaz on a Remote Manipulator System (RMS) performs work on the ISS; *right,* Expedition 64 Flight Engineer Victor Glover works on a plant water management experiment.

Engineer Colin Creager attaches the latest version of the SuperElastic SMA (Shape Memory Alloy) Spring Tire used on the Mars rover, which will be used on the VIPER Moon rover *(right)*.

Top right, NASA technicians finish applying more than 180 blocks of thermal protection to *Orion*'s heat shield.

Volatiles Investigating Polar Exploration Rover (VIPER)

NASA is currently building its own lunar rover, called VIPER. It is designed to locate water ice on the Moon, then to select the best places to retrieve it. The rover will help NASA pick out landing spots for Artemis III and future missions. Being near a source of water is extremely important for the future inhabitants of the Moon. Companies on Earth are already working on ways to extract the water ice and make it drinkable.

Do you like to solve mechanical problems? Test the wheels on Mars rovers. Want to figure out if there really is water ice on the Moon or Mars? Study hydrology or geology.

Worried about whether astronauts will get back home safely without getting overheated? Become a thermal engineer.

Moonikin on Board

The Artemis I mission did not include humans in the *Orion* spacecraft. It did, however, include a mannequin, Commander Moonikin Campos by name. Commander Campos looks like a crash-test dummy found in cars. Why is it on board the *Orion* spacecraft?

Since the *Orion* spacecraft is destined to fly the farthest a human has ever flown from Earth, it's important for scientists to understand the amount of radiation a person might experience. The moonikin is equipped with special sensors, which also track the amount of acceleration (G-forces) and vibration that happens in the capsule during transit. Commander Campos is also wearing the next-generation *Orion* suit, which, in addition to being sporty, allows NASA to test the suit in advance of astronauts wearing it.

Commander Moonikin Campos, mannequin aboard the Orion spacecraft during Artemis I.

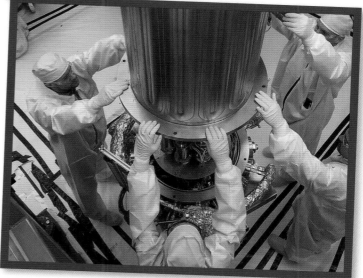

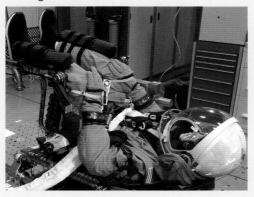

Top right, Rory Rosselot adjusts hardware in front of mini-pixel chamber at the NASA Space Radiation Laboratory (NSRL); *bottom right*, engineers lower the wall of a vacuum chamber into the new fission surface power project planned for use on the Moon.

Are you interested in space medicine? As a medical doctor, you could study the effects of radiation on the human body in space.

Curious about nuclear power? Perhaps you can help design a nuclear fusion device that could power the base on the Moon.

Fusion energy is the energy of the future! At least that's what many people on this planet hope. It promises a huge amount of energy without any toxic side effects.

179

Left, high school students participating in NASA's HUNCH Culinary Program create food for astronauts on the ISS; *right,* Barb Tewksbury, geologist at Hamilton College, works with an astronaut to understand the study of geology.

Do you like to create food and set up menus? Food chemists and dieticians are needed to make those in-flight meals tastier!

But you don't need to be interested in science to work at a space agency or commercial space company. The growing space economy needs people with all kinds of interests.

Like to draw? Design advertisements for space travel companies or space agencies.

Interested in being a tour guide to the stars? Organize excursions for tourists to LEO.

How about fashion? Join a team that's designing a form-fitting, knitted biosuit.

Want to help get kids excited about space? Write a book! Compose music for a video.

Or if setting policy and making decisions is more your thing, you could help solve those knotty conundrums. How?

Study economics to help non-spacefaring nations get involved in space.

Learn languages that are foreign to you.

Work at the United Nations.

Run for Congress or the legislature in your country to develop space-friendly policies.

Become a diplomat.

Or a lawyer.

With a law degree, become a judge at the International Court of Justice.

A journalist covering launches.

Left, Senator Jeanne Shaheen (D-NH) gives remarks as NASA astronauts Victor Glover and Reid Wiseman look on during a meet and greet in Washington, DC, in 2023; *right,* collaboration between Friendswood High School art students and the NASA Johnson Space Center team to create and display a new mural.

A teacher, sharing your excitement about both the engineering and the policies needed to support life in space.

A peacemaker.

Does this seem like it's too far in your future? Actually, you don't have to wait! You can do something right now. Helping others learn more about space and getting involved in your own world can happen at any time. Not sure where to start?

Explore career paths for kids at NASA on this website: nasa.gov/learning-resources/.

Intern at the European Space Agency. Apply to the International Telecommunication Union's Youth Advisory Board.

Or talk with astronauts on the ISS via Amateur Radio on the International Space Station (ARISS)—ariss.org.

Track objects in the night sky with a telescope and report what you see to Astriagraph.

Become a citizen scientist. Love science? You can help. Anyone can be a citizen scientist. There are *tons* of ways to get involved with NASA. You could enter one of the agency's many contests like these: design new ways to create power for spacecraft, count trees around the Earth, or spot clouds on Mars. You could watch exoplanets, or track asteroids, or even become a dark-energy explorer! (science.nasa.gov/citizenscience)

The list of careers relating to space is endless. One of the exciting features

Space Lawyers

Multiple law schools in the US and abroad have specialties in space law. You could look into the University of Connecticut, the University of Nebraska, Georgetown University, the University of Mississippi, Leiden University, McGill University, ESA's European Centre for Space Law, the Institute of Air and Space Law in Germany, the University of Sydney in Australia—and more.

Making Peace

There are actually programs around the world that help people and groups reduce conflict and foster peace. You could look at the Jimmy and Rosalyn Carter School for Peace and Conflict Resolution at George Mason University, Peace Studies at Georgetown University, International Peace Studies at the University of Notre Dame, the School of International Studies at Johns Hopkins University, the University of Oslo, Uppsala University, the University of Cape Town, Rotary International's Peace Fellowships, and others.

about these fields is that they combine a fun mix of skills and knowledge:

- geography + drawing
- civics + travel
- geology + sculpture
- chemistry + food
- statistics + policy
- social studies + astronomy

Concoct a mash-up of your favorite activities and interests and see how they might work for you in an area related to space. The need for critical thinkers and problem solvers is always there. Just remember to use your creativity as well.

Finally, be curious and thoughtful. We encourage you to expand your knowledge about the topics covered in this book. Then turn your curiosity into action.

Consider becoming a part of history by helping to solve one of these conundrums, discovering a new way to power a spacecraft, or making your very own footprints on the Moon. The possibilities of space exploration—like your curiosity—are infinite.

Whatever you decide, know that you will grow up in a world where people may be living on, and near, other celestial bodies besides Earth. The world as you know it is about to get much, much larger, and it will need amazingly curious, critical thinkers like you to explore and solve the problems of the future.

Space is for everybody. It's not just for a few people in math or science, or for a select group of astronauts. That's our new frontier out there, and it's everybody's business to know about space.

—Christa McAuliffe

ACRONYMS

AKM: apogee kick motor
ARISS: Amateur Radio on the International
   Space Station
ASAT: Anti-satellite; also short for anti-satellite
   weapon
CSA: Canadian Space Agency
CNSA: Chinese National Space Administration
COPUOS: Committee on the Peaceful Uses of
   Outer Space
COSPAR: Committee on Space Research
ESA: European Space Agency
FAA: Federal Aviation Administration
FAI: Fédération Aéronautique Internationale
FBI: Federal Bureau of Investigation
FCC: Federal Communications Commission
GEO: Geostationary (geosynchronous
   equatorial) orbit
GMT: Greenwich Mean Time
GPS: Global Positioning System
GSO: Geosynchronous orbit
HALO: habitation and logistics outpost
HEO: high Earth orbit
HLS: Human Landing System
IADC: Inter-Agency Space Debris Coordination
   Committee
ICBM: intercontinental ballistic missile
ICJ: International Court of Justice
ISRO: Indian Space Research Organisation
ISS: International Space Station
ITU: International Telecommunication Union
JAXA: Japan Aerospace Exploration Agency
KA-SAT: Viasat telecommunication satellite
   network
LEO: low Earth orbit

LTV: Lunar Terrain Vehicle
MEO: medium Earth orbit
MEV: Mission Extension Vehicle
MILAMOS: Manual on International Law
   Applicable to Military Uses of Outer Space
MRP: Mission Refueling Pod
MRV: Mission Robotic Vehicle
NASA: National Aeronautics and Space
   Administration
NOAA: National Oceanic and Atmospheric
   Administration
NRO: National Reconnaissance Office
ORBITS: Orbital Sustainability Act
OSHA: Occupational Safety and Health
   Administration
OST: Outer Space Treaty
PPE: power and propulsion element
PPWT: Prevention of the Placement of
   Weapons in Outer Space
RPO: rendezvous and proximity operations
SIGINT: signals intelligence
SLS: Space Launch System
SSN: Space Surveillance Network
ULA: United Launch Alliance
UN: United Nations
UNOOSA: United Nations Office for Outer
   Space Affairs
USSR: Union of Soviet Socialist Republics
UV: ultraviolet
VAB: Vehicle Assembly Building
VLEO: very low Earth orbit
VIPER: Volatiles Investigating Polar Exploration
   Rover
WMD: weapons of mass destruction

A NOTE FROM THE AUTHORS

People often ask why we chose to team up to write this book. After all, we are both pretty well-known for our own books and areas of expertise—Cynthia writes about history, law, politics, and the arts, and Jennifer writes about science, technology, engineering, math, and history. So why did we collaborate?

The material presented in this book is complex and required a great deal of research and organization to craft it into a cohesive message. What would have been a huge task for one person was made much easier by pooling our collective knowledge of and passion for these topics. The result is *Who Owns the Moon?* — an in-depth look at the issues that surround living and working in low Earth orbit and the possible establishment of a base on the Moon. We have learned so much and worked hard during our three-year journey together. We hope you have found this book as informative and thought-provoking to read as we found it to write.

Our greatest wish is that reading it will have engaged your curiosity, ignited your imagination, and stimulated your creativity. We would love for this book to spur you to learn more about space technology, space policy, space law, and space science.

After all, YOU are the future of our planet. Your generation will set policy, make laws, invent the technologies, and provide the motivation and sheer determination to take us beyond Earth's atmosphere. You have the power to establish our place in the universe.

Ad astra!
Jennifer and
Cynthia

ACKNOWLEDGMENTS

When you have a lot to learn, you also have many people to thank for teaching you. We are indebted to multiple scientists, engineers, astronauts, lawyers, historians, government officials, writers, business people, and others for their patient and thorough explanations. Above all, we are infinitely grateful to the following individuals for generously reading, correcting, and improving drafts of the book-in-progress: authors Gail Jarrow and Laurie Wallmark; lawyers Michelle Hanlon, Steve Mirmina, and Ruth Stilwell; former Secretary of the Navy Richard J. Danzig; and teachers Suzanne Costner, Jeff Gonyea, and Cassondra Zielinski.

But for the editorial and design team at Peachtree Publishers and Margaret Quinlin Books, this book would not be the beautiful and inspiring production you hold. We are inordinately grateful to our editor, Margaret Quinlin; designer Trish Parcell; photo editor Kelly Loughman; illustrators Thomas Gonzalez and Ed Miller; copy editor George Newman; and copy editor/proofreader Pamela Day. Our great appreciation, too, goes to Aimee Crane, Tyrone McCoy, and Connie Moore at NASA; John Bateman at NOAA; Sarah Grover at the Polaris Program; Jeff Michael at Virgin Atlantic; Kim Persse at Space Perspective; Shannon Whetzel at the Cosmosphere, Hutchinson, Kansas; and Kate Igoe, Kay Peterson, and Erik Satrum at the Smithsonian for their kind assistance with visuals. Cynthia and Jennifer would also like to thank their agents, Erin Murphy and Lori Kilkelly, respectively, who helped keep this book on track from concept to completion.

In addition, Cynthia deeply thanks the following experts for personally answering her innumerable questions: aerospace engineer Moriba Jah; astrophysicist Martin Elvis; physicist Kai Lee; astronaut William Shepherd; astronaut trainer Ginger Kerrick; author William Causey; entrepreneur Andrew Rothgaber; lawyers Mark K. Craig, Diane Howard, Brian Israel, Derek Jinks, Matthew Kleiman, David A. Koplow, Elsbeth Magilton, Laura Montgomery, Kai-Uwe Schrogl, Milton Smith, Michael Sturley, Mark Sundahl, and Ellen Vargas; professors Hélène Landemore, John Logsdon, Larry F. Martinez, and Frans von der Dunk; NASA policymaker Bhavya Lal; pilot Josh Granof; and Presidential Librarians Mary Burtzloff and Ariel Turley.

Cynthia's daughters, sons-in-law, and grandchildren are as thoroughly splendid as ever. (Special shoutout to Eli and Sarah, who helpfully critiqued a few chapters!)—CL

Many thanks to all the experts who helped me with this book. And of course, huge thanks to my dear friends and family, without whose love and support I couldn't write any of the books I do, especially this one. You all ROCK!—JS

The publisher sends heartfelt thanks to this wonderful team of collaborators who supported the authors and me throughout the development of *Who Owns the Moon?*: Trish Parcell, Kelly Loughman, and Pam Day. Each of you made a significant impact on the book. I am so grateful.—MQ

PICTURE CREDITS

Album/Alamy Stock Photo: 20
Alejandro Miranda/Alamy: 99
Archive.org: 10 ("Red's Lunik Hits the Moon" by Universal Studios, Universal Newsreels collection, dedicated to the public domain via Creative Commons.)
Blue Origin: 120 *(top)*
Christophe Coat/Alamy Stock Photo: 13
ClearSpace SA: 109
Corbis Historical/Getty Images: 31
Cosmosphere: 18 (Lunasphere image courtesy of the Cosmosphere, Hutchinson, Kansas)
Department of Defense via UPI/Alamy: 49
Edward Miller: 44, 49 (inset), 83, 86, 93, 167–171 (astronauts)
ESA: 90–91
ESA/NASA: 95 (Timothy Peake)
Everett Collection Historical/Alamy: 14, 18 (top)
Inspiration4 Crew: 117
Library of Congress (LC-USZ62-71278): 126
NASA: vi, 1–7, 16 (Sputnik), 17, 25, 28, 33, 40, 54, 57, 60, 62–63, 64-65, 67, 69, 76, 79, 80–81, 96–97, 121 (bottom), 128–145, 148–149, 177–181

NASA Image Collection/Alamy Stock Photo: 60
National Anthropological Archives, Smithsonian Institution (OCA-WI JN2018-01447): 15
National Archives CIARDP78TO3194A000200050001-8: 19
NOAA: 42
National Reconnaissance Office: 110
Patricia Parcell: *timelines* 8, 22–23; *maps* 12, 46–47, 73, 103; *other* 10
The Protected Art Archive/Alamy: 20
Rachid Darbali-Zamora et al.: 83 (CubeSat Design. See Chapter 6 source notes for full reference.)
Roberto Michel/Alamy: 85 (bottom)
Shutterstock: 10 (audience)
SpaceX: 84
Space Perspectives: 121 (top)
Stocktrek Images, Inc./Alamy: 77
Tom Gonzalez: *lunar landscapes* i–v, 8–9, 22–23, 36, 39, 51, 53, 64–65, 74, 82, 102, 107, 114–115, 147, 150, 162–163; *lunar regolith spots* 41, 74, 82, 102, 150, 164, 176; *other illustrations* 36, 174–175,183–185
Wikipedia: 16 (inset)

SOURCE NOTES

Introduction
PAGE
3   "This is an extraordinary day...new generation": William Harwood, "Artemis moonship returns to Earth with picture-perfect Pacific Ocean splashdown," CBS News, December 11, 2022. *https://www.cbsnews.com/news/artemis-1-orion-splashdown-watch-live-stream-today-12-11-2022/*

4   "We choose to go to the Moon...because they are hard": President John F. Kennedy, "Address at Rice University on the Nation's Space Effort," September 12, 1962. *https://www.jfklibrary.org/archives/other-resources/john-f-kennedy-speeches/rice-university-19620912*

6   "The exploration and use...province of all mankind." Article I of the Outer Space Treaty, United Nations Office of Outer Space Affairs, December 1, 1966. *https://www.unoosa.org/oosa/en/ourwork/spacelaw/treaties/outerspacetreaty.html*

Chapter 1
PAGE
11   "Soviet Russia...hit the Moon!": International Astronautical Federation, "Red's 'Lunik' Hits the Moon," Universal Newsreel, September 14, 1959. *https://www.youtube.com/watch?v=Osfs3AnH-ZA*

11   "Bearing the Soviet...body to another" :ibid.

11   "almost dead on target": ibid.

11   "propaganda bonus...to America": ibid.

18   "Americans sleep under a Soviet Moon": "The Space Race," *Digital History* (blog ID 3426). *https://www.digitalhistory.uh.edu/disp_textbook.cfm?smtid=2&psid=3426#*

18   "the Soviet Union...moon sovereignty": Peter Khiss, "U.S. Rejects Any Flag-Planting As Legal Claim to Rule Moon," *New York Times*, September 14, 1959. *https://www.nytimes.com/1959/09/14/archives/us-rejects-any-flagplanting-as-legal-claim-to-rule-moon-us-rejects.html*

21   "the exploration and use of outer space...for peaceful purposes": Committee on the Peaceful Uses of Outer Space. *https://www.unoosa.org/oosa/en/ourwork/copuos/index.html*

Chapter 2
PAGE
24   "[a] group of us...across town": Jade Boyd, "JFK's 1962 moon speech still appeals 50 years later," Rice University News and Media Relations, August 30, 2012. *https://news.rice.edu/news/2012/jfks-1962-moon-speech-still-appeals-50-years-later*

24   "I clearly remember...with skinny ties": Sam Byrd, "Reflecting on President Kennedy's 'Moonshot' speech 60 years later," Rice University News and Media Relations, September 6, 2022. *https://news.rice.edu/news/2022/reflecting-president-kennedys-moonshot-speech-60-years-later*

24   "We meet at a college...age of both knowledge and ignorance": President John F. Kennedy, "Address at Rice University on the Nation's Space Effort," September 12, 1962. *https://www.jfklibrary.org/archives/other-resources/john-f-kennedy-speeches/rice-university-19620912*

24   "We choose to go to the Moon...we intend to win": ibid.

26   "launch a piloted...back to earth": Stephen J. Garber, "The Friendship 7 Mission: A Major Achievement and a Sign of More to Come," NASA.gov. *https://history.nasa.gov/friendship7/*

28 "We shall not see it governed...of freedom and peace": Anne M. Platoff, "Where No Flag Has Gone Before: Political and Technical Aspects of Placing a Flag on the Moon," Paper presented to the 26th Meeting of the North American Vexillological Association, October 11, 1992. *https://historycollection.jsc.nasa.gov/JSCHistoryPortal/history/flag/flag.htm*

29 "no matter how small...with the greatest Powers": Stephen Buono, "Merely a 'Scrap of Paper'? The Outer Space Treaty in Historical Perspective." *Diplomacy & Statecraft*, 31:2 (2020), pp. 350–372. *https://doi.org/10.1080/09592296.2020.1760038*

30 "Space is a frontier...humanity acting in concert": Lyndon B. Johnson, "Remarks at Ceremony Marking the Entry Into Force of the Outer Space Treaty," October 10, 1967. *https://www.presidency.ucsb.edu/documents/remarks-ceremony-marking-the-entry-into-force-the-outer-space-treaty*

30 "the treaty...among states and people": ibid.

32 "Houston, Tranquility...smooth touchdown": "Voice From Moon: 'Eagle Has Landed,'" *New York Times*, July 21, 1969. *https://timesmachine.nytimes.com/timesmachine/1969/07/21/issue.html*

32 "That's one small step...leap for mankind": "Armstrong's famous 'one small step' quote—explained," Associated Press, July 10, 2019. *https://apnews.com/article/business-science-apollo-11-moon-landing-29f856124ea540f6ba00bee1ddf6d4d9Bu*

32 "It's a great honor...peace of all nations": John Noble Wilford, "A Powdery Surface Is Closely Explored," *New York Times*, July 21, 1969. *https://timesmachine.nytimes.com/timesmachine/1969/07/21/issue.html*

Chapter 4
PAGE

54 "Six meters. Five. Four.": Clare Lewins, *The Wonderful: Stories from the Space Station*, Universal Pictures and Dog Star Films, April 2021.

54 "Three...arrived": ibid.

55 "Somebody has...the lights": ibid.

55 "It was...we were scrambling": ibid.

55 "We're in contact": ibid.

55 "We are the...one for Houston": "First ISS Commander Reflects on Station's 10th Anniversary," September 14, 2010. *https://www.youtube.com/watch?v=Rg-eVs1A_p8*

55 "That was...day in space": "International Space Station Expedition 1: The Beginning," October 29, 2020. *https://www.youtube.com/watch?v=tgl7uKC4rJk*

56 "with other nations and groups of nations": Public Law 85-568.

58 "shall comply...management policies": 14 CFR Section 1214.403 – Code of Conduct for the International Space Station Crew. *https://www.law.cornell.edu/cfr/text/14/1214.403*

59 "The only way...talk to them": "First ISS Commander Reflects on Station's 10th Anniversary," September 14, 2010. *https://www.youtube.com/watch?v=Rg-eVs1A_p8*

59 "Without the Russians...a space station": William Shepherd, interview by Zoom, April 11, 2022.

Chapter 5
PAGE

66 "We deeply deplore...imposed on Russia": "No 9-2022: ExoMars suspended," European Space Agency, 17 March 2022. *https://www.esa.int/Newsroom/Press_Releases/ExoMars_suspended*

66 "If you block...into the United States": @Rogozin, via Twitter Translate, Loren Grush, February 24, 2022. *https://twitter.com/lorengrush/status/1496938103570845699?t=3ccdV-b6-UTlb6fn0zxPTA&s=19*

69 "The ISS project...be out of politics": Marcia Smith, "Borisov Clarifies Russia's Space Station Plans," Spacepolicyonline.com, July 29, 2022. *https://spacepolicyonline.com/news/borisov-clarifies-russias-space-station-plans/*

74 "be used...of all mankind": Antarctic Treaty. *https://2009-2017.state.gov/t/avc/trty/193967.htm*

75 "To explore...our eternal dream": President Xi Jinping, "China's Space Program: A 2021 Perspective," China National Space Administration, January 28, 2022. *http://www.cnsa.gov.cn/english/n6465652/n6465653/c6813088/content.html*

76 "I realized that...exciting findings": Kenneth Chang, "Scientists Have Found a

Hot Spot on the Moon's Far Side," *New York Times*, July 12, 2023. *https://www.nytimes.com/2023/07/11/science/moon-hot-spot-granite.html*

77   "The United States…of the Red Planet": Ed Browne, "NASA Boss Bill Nelson Says China 'Aggressive Competitor' After Mars Landing," *Newsweek*, May 20, 2021. *https//www.newsweek.com/nasa-bill-nelson-china-competitor-mars-rover-moon-landings-planning-1593241*

77   "a very aggressive competitor": Aristos Georgiou, "NASA Wants to Work With China in Space," *Newsweek*, September 24, 2021. *https://www.newsweek.com/nasa-administrator-bill-nelson-work-china-1632508*

77   "I wish China…have been": ibid.

Chapter 6
PAGE

83   CubeSat design from Darbali-Zamora, Rachid & Merced, Daniel & Gonzalez-Ortiz, Cesar & Ortiz-Rivera, Eduardo. (2014). An Electric Power Supply design for the space plasma ionic charge analyzer (SPICA) CubeSat. 1790-1795. 10.1109/PVSC.2014.6925270.

Chapter 7
PAGE

92   "Thanks for a crazy…you gave us": Meghan Bartels, "Space debris forces astronauts on space station to take shelter in return ships," Space.com, November 15, 2012. *https://www.space.com/space-debris-astronauts-shelter-november-2021*

92   "It was…as a crew": ibid.

94   "any human-made…from completed missions": NASA Science Editorial Team, "10 Things: What's That Space Rock?" NASA.gov, July 21, 2022. *https://www.nasa.gov/mission_pages/station/news/orbital_debris.html*

95   "This is the chip…quadruple glazed!": Tim Peake, "Impact Chip," European Space Agency, May 12, 2016. *https://www.esa.int/ESA_Multimedia/Images/2016/05/Impact_chip*

97   "to avert a catastrophe": Marcia Smith, "NASA Safety Panel Issues Clarion Call for ISS Deorbit Tug," Spacepolicyonline.com, October 26, 2023. *https://spacepolicyonline.com/news/nasa-safety-panel-issues-clarion-call-for-iss-deorbit-tug/*

98   "It's going to…no stoplights": Tereza Pultarova, "How many satellites can we safely fit in Earth orbit?" Space.com, February 27, 2023. *https://www.space.com/how-many-satellites-fit-safely-earth-orbit*

98   "complete disregard…of space": Jeff Foust, "Russia destroys satellite in ASAT. test," Spacenews.com, November 15, 2021 *https://spacenews.com/russia-destroys-satellite-in-asat-test/*

109   "clearly capable…maneuver[ing]": Theresa Hitchens, "China's SJ-21 'tugs' dead satellite out of GEO belt: Trackers," Breaking Defense, January 26, 2022. *https://breaking-defense.com/2022/01/chinas-sj-21-tugs-dead-satellite-out-of-geo-belt-trackers/*

Chapter 9
PAGE

116   "Are you…under way": Inspiration4, "Super Bowl Ad: Join The First All-Civilian Space Mission/Inspiration 4," February 3, 2021. *https://www.youtube.com/watch?v=_nwSmOEiDls*

116   "This fall…to space": ibid.

116   "That's…opportunity": Jason Hehir, *Countdown, Inspiration4 Mission to Space*, Netflix, 2021. *https://www.netflix.com/watch /81462385?trackId=155573558_*

116   "making humankind a multiplanetary species": Christian Davenport, "Jared Isaacman, who led the first all-private astronaut mission to orbit, has commissioned 3 more flights from SpaceX," *Washington Post*, February 14, 2022. *https://www.washingtonpost.com/technology/2022/02/14/jared-isaacman-polaris-spacex-starship-inspiration4/*

117   "We're changing…to space": Jason Hehir, *Countdown, Inspiration4 Mission to Space*, Netflix, 2021. *https://www.netflix.com/watch/81462387?trackId=155573560*

119   "the chance...a reality": Wally Funk and Loretta Hall, "Outtakes from Wally's Memoir," Wallyfly.com. *https://wallyfly.com/Outtakes.html*

122   "Earth light": Frank Buckley, "Dr. Sian Proctor and the Future of Space Tourism/Frank Buckley Interviews," KTLA 5, March 25, 2023. *https://www.youtube.com/watch?v=SlCtdmTCxOA*

126   "It's all I've ever wanted": "The Next Astronauts Part IV: Risk," Axios podcast, September 14, 2021. *https://www.axios.com/2021/09/14/next-astronauts-part-four_*

127   "The United States...spaceflight participants": Code of Federal Regulations, Section 460.9 – Informing crew of risk. *https://www.ecfr.gov/current/title-14/chapter-III/subchapter-C/part-460*

Chapter 10
PAGE

132   "We're going back...benefit of all": "Why We're Going to the Moon," NASA.gov. *https://www.nasa.gov/feature/artemis/#*

142   "a voice in the wilderness": "John C. Houbolt, Unsung Hero of the Apollo Program, Dies at Age 95," Moon Daily, April 22, 2014. *https://www.moondaily.com/reports/John_C_Houbolt_Unsung_Hero_of_the_Apollo_Program_Dies_at_Age_95_999.html*

Chapter 11
PAGE

148   "This is certainly different": Chelsea Gohd, "The touchscreen controls of SpaceX's Crew Dragon give astronauts a sci-fi way to fly in space," Space.com, May 29, 2020. *https://www.space.com/spacex-crew-dragon-touchscreen-astronaut-thoughts.html*

149   "Welcome...SpaceX": Nell Greenfieldboyce, "Splashdown! SpaceX and NASA Astronauts Make History," NPR, August 2, 2020. *https://www.npr.org/2020/08/02/898330964/splashdown-spacex-and-nasa-astronauts-make-history*

152   "obtrusive space advertising": 51 USC 50911: Space advertising. *http://uscode.house.gov/view.xhtml?req=granuleid:USC-prelim-title5-section50911&num=0&edition=prelim*

153   "a sovereign...beings": "Declaration of the Rights of the Moon," Draft for circulation and discussion version, February 11, 2021. *https://www.earthlaws.org.au/moon-declaration/*

154   "We will...lunar quest": ispace, "ispace HAKUTO-R Mission 1: Landing Live Stream," April 25, 2023. *https://www.youtube.com/watch?v=CpR1UUnix3g*

156   "delivery in place": Frans von der Dunk, "The Future is Now: Issues in Space Law and Policy," Presentation at "Issues in Space Law and Policy," Washington, DC, October 12, 2022.

157   "invasion": Michael Byers and Aaron Boley, *Who Owns Outer Space? International Law, Astrophysics, and the Sustainable Development of Space* (New York: Cambridge University Press, 2023), p. 160.

Chapter 12
PAGE

164   "Policy can...rocket science": Robin Dickey, Panel on "Responsible Stewardship of the Moon," Conference on "Issues in Space Law and Policy," Washington, DC, October 12, 2022.

Chapter 13
PAGE

183   "Space is for...about space": Christa McAuliffe, "Space Quotes," Sea and Sky Presents: The Sky. *http://www.seasky.org/quotes/space-quotes.html#*

FURTHER READING, VIEWING, AND DOING

Books

Maurer, Richard. *Destination Moon: The Remarkable and Improbable Voyage of Apollo 11*. New York: Roaring Brook Press, 2019.

Rocco, John. *How We Got to the Moon: The People, Technology, and Daring Feats of Science Behind Humanity's Greatest Adventure*. New York: Crown Books for Young Readers, 2020.

Slade, Suzanne. *Countdown: 2979 Days to the Moon*. Illustrated by Thomas Gonzalez. Atlanta: Peachtree Publishers, 2018.

Swanson, Jennifer. *Spacecare: A Kid's Guide to Surviving Space*. Washington, DC: Mayo Clinic Press/Smithsonian Institution, 2023.

Weinersmith, Kelly, and Zach Weinersmith. *A City on Mars: Can We Settle Space, Should We Settle Space, and Have We Really Thought This Through?* New York: Penguin Press, 2023.

Films

"First ISS Commander [William Shepherd] Reflects on Station's 10th Anniversary." October 27, 2010. YouTube video, 27:25. *https://www.youtube.com /watch?v=Rg-eVs1A_p8&ab_channel=NASA*.

"International Space Station Expedition 1: The Beginning." October 29, 2020. YouTube video (with Jeanne Meserve, William Shepherd, Ginger Karrick, Yuri Gidzenko, Sergei Krikalev, and George Abbey), 45:02. *https://www.youtube .com/watch?v=3OpDe4v9MbI&ab _channel=NASA*.

Lewins, Clare, director. *The Wonderful: Stories from the Space Station*. Universal Pictures and Dog Star Films, April 2021. 2 hr. 7min.

Podcasts

Houston We Have a Podcast. From Earth orbit to the Moon and Mars, explore the world of human spaceflight with NASA each week on the official podcast of the Johnson Space Center in Houston, Texas. *https://www.nasa .gov/podcasts/houston-we-have-a-podcast/*

Solve It! for Kids. Episodes chatting with numerous astronauts, engineers from NASA, Lockheed Martin, Boeing, and many more, as they share their amazing jobs. Each episode ends with a challenge for the listeners. *https://solveitforkids.com/*

NASA's Curious Universe. Our universe is a wild and wonderful place. Join NASA astronauts, scientists, and engineers on a new adventure each episode—all you need is your curiosity! *https://www.nasa.gov/podcasts/curious -universe/*

Universo curioso de la NASA. Bienvenidos a Universo curioso de la NASA, en donde te invitamos a explorar el cosmos en tu idioma. En este pódcast, ¡la NASA es tu guía turística a las estrellas! *https://www.nasa.gov /podcasts/universo-curioso-de-la-nasa/*

NASA's Small Steps, Giant Leaps. NASA's technical workforce put boots on the Moon, tire tracks on Mars, and the first reusable spacecraft in orbit around the Earth. Learn what's next as they build missions that redefine the future with amazing discoveries and remarkable innovations. *https://www .nasa.gov/podcasts/small-steps-giant-leaps/*

Sites to Visit

Goddard Visitor Center, Greenbelt, Maryland *(https://www.nasa.gov/goddard/visitor-center/)*

Johnson Space Center, Houston, Texas *(https://www.nasa.gov/johnson/)*

Kennedy Space Center, Merritt Island, Florida *(https://www.kennedyspacecenter.com/)*

Marshall Space Flight Center, Huntsville, Alabama *(https://www.nasa.gov/marshall/)*

Smithsonian National Air and Space Museum, Washington, DC *(https://airandspace.si.edu/)*

Steven F. Udvar-Hazy Center (Smithsonian National Air and Space Museum Annex), Washington Dulles International Airport, Chantilly, Virginia. *(https://airandspace.si.edu/visit/udvar-hazy-center)*

US Space & Rocket Center, Huntsville, Alabama. *(https://www.rocketcenter.com/)*

Websites

Artemis Accords: *https://www.nasa.gov/artemis-accords/*

Astriagraph: *http://astria.tacc.utexas.edu/AstriaGraph/*

Boeing: *https://www.boeing.com/*

Blue Origin: *https://www.blueorigin.com/*

European Space Agency: *https://www.esa.int/*

For All Moonkind: *https://www.forallmoonkind.org/*

Kennedy Space Center: *https://www.kennedyspacecenter.com/*

Lockheed Martin Space: *https://www.lockheedmartin.com/en-us/capabilities/space.html*

MIT Space Exploration Initiative: *https://www.explore-space.mit.edu/*

National Aeronautics and Space Administration (NASA): *https://www.nasa.gov/*

SpaceX: *https://www.spacex.com/*

Treaty on Principles Governing the Activities of States in the Exploration and Use of Outer Space, including the Moon and Other Celestial Bodies: *https://www.unoosa.org/oosa/en/ourwork/spacelaw/treaties/outerspacetreaty.html*

Wayfinder: *https://wayfinder.privateer.com/*

SELECTED BIBLIOGRAPHY

If we cited every single source we used to research and verify all of the information in *Who Owns the Moon?* (which we considered doing), you would need a wheelbarrow to cart the book around. Instead, we're listing here our major go-to sources. Use these, along with the resources we listed in "Further Reading, Viewing, and Doing," to delve into the topics that you find intriguing. The universe is yours to explore, and it begins here.

Books

Byers, Michael, and Aaron Boley. *Who Owns Space? International Law, Astrophysics, and the Sustainable Development of Space.* New York: Cambridge University Press, 2023.

Chaikin, Andrew. *A Man on the Moon, Vol. I: One Giant Leap.* New York: Time Life Books, 1999.

Elvis, Martin. *Asteroids: How Love, Fear, and Greed Will Determine Our Future in Space.* New Haven: Yale University Press, 2021.

Johnson, Christopher D., ed. *Handbook for New Actors in Space.* Secure World Foundation, 2017.

Kleiman, Matthew J. *The Little Book of Space Law.* American Bar Association, 2013.

Maurer, Richard. *Destination Moon: The Remarkable and Improbable Voyage of Apollo 11.* New York: Roaring Brook Press, 2019.

Mirmina, Steve and Caryn Schenewerk. *International Space Law and Space Laws of the United States.* Northampton: Edward Elgar Publishing, 2022.

Sivolella, Davide. *Space Mining and Manufacturing: Off-World Resources and Revolutionary Engineering Techniques.* Chichester: Springer/Praxis Books, 2019.

Steer, Cassandra, and Matthew Hersch. *War and Peace in Outer Space: Law, Policy, and Ethics.* New York: Oxford University Press, 2021.

Teitel, Amy Shira. *Breaking the Chains of Gravity: The Story of Spaceflight before NASA.* New York: Bloomsbury Publishing, 2016.

von der Dunk, Frans G. *Advanced Introduction to Space Law.* Northampton: Edward Elgar Publishing, 2020.

von der Dunk, Frans G. *Handbook of Space Law.* Northampton: Edward Elgar Publishing, 2015.

Weinersmith, Kelly, and Zach Weinersmith. *A City on Mars: Can We Settle Space, Should We Settle Space, and Have We Really Thought This Through?* New York: Penguin Press, 2023.

Wouters, Jan, Philip De Man, and Rik Hansen, eds. *Commercial Uses of Space and Space Tourism: Legal and Policy Aspects.* Northampton: Edward Elgar Publishing, 2017.

Films

"First ISS Commander [William Shepherd] Reflects on Station's 10th Anniversary." October 27, 2010. YouTube video, 27:25. *https://www.youtube.com/watch?v=Rg-eVs1A_p8&ab_channel=NASA*

"International Space Station Expedition 1: The Beginning." October 29, 2020.

YouTube video (with Jeanne Meserve, William Shepherd, Ginger Karrick, Yuri Gidzenko, Sergei Krikalev, and George Abbey), 45:02. *https://www.youtube.com/watch?v=3OpDe4v9MbI&ab_channel=NASA*

Lewins, Clare, director. *The Wonderful: Stories from the Space Station.* Universal Pictures and Dog Star Films, April 2021. 2 hr., 7 min.

Interviews

Burtzloff, Mary—Archivist, Eisenhower Presidential Library

Causey, William F.—Author

Coleman, Cady—Astronaut

Craig, Mark K.—Former NASA engineer

Danzig, Richard J.—Former Secretary of the Navy

Elvis, Martin—Astrophysicist, Harvard University

Granof, Josh—Pilot

Hanlon, Michelle—Space lawyer, University of Mississippi

Howard, Diane—Director, Commercial Space Policy at the National Space Council

Jah, Moriba—Aerospace engineer and assistant professor, University of Texas at Austin

Jinks, Derek—A.W. Walker Centennial Chair in Law, University of Texas at Austin

Kerrick, Ginger—ISS astronaut trainer

Kleiman, Matthew—Author and CEO of Cumulous Digital Systems

Koplow, David A.—National Security lawyer, Georgetown Law

Lal, Bhavya—Former Associate Administrator for Technology, Policy, and Strategy, NASA

Lee, Kai—Physicist

Logsdon, John M.—Professor, George Washington University

Magilton, Elsbeth—Space lawyer, Nebraska College of Law

Mirmina, Steve—Space lawyer, NASA

Montgomery, Laura—Space lawyer, Catholic University

Ramon, Lou—Engineer, NASA

Rothgaber, Andrew—ICON

Shepherd, William—Astronaut

Smith, Milton—Space lawyer, Sherman & Howard Law Firm

Stilwell, Ruth—Space lawyer, Norwich University

Sturley, Michael F.—Maritime lawyer, University of Texas at Austin

Sundahl, Mark J.—Space lawyer, Cleveland State University

Tucker, Britt—*Blue Origin*

Turley, Ariel—Archivist, Eisenhower Presidential Library

Vargyas, Ellen—Lawyer, American Legacy Foundation

von der Dunk, Frans G.—Historian, Nebraska College of Law

Organizations and Media Outlets

Aerospace Center for Space Policy and Strategy

Axios Space and Axios/Science/Space

Beyond Earth Institute

Boeing

International Academy of Astronautics (IAA)

International Institute of Space Law (IISL)

International Space Station Research and Development Conference (ISSRDC)

Lockheed Martin Space

National Space Society (NSS)

Payload

Secure World Foundation

Space Café Global

Space Policy Institute

Space Policy Online

SpaceX

The Strauss Center for International Security and Law

Treaties, Laws, Regulations, Accords, and United Nations Documents

Agreement Governing the Activities of States on the Moon and Other Celestial Bodies (also known as the Moon Treaty or Moon Agreement)

Agreement on the Rescue of Astronauts, the Return of Astronauts and the Return of Objects Launched into Outer Space (also known as the Rescue Agreement)

Artemis Accords

Convention on International Liability for Damage Caused by Space Objects

Convention on Registration of Objects
Launched into Outer Space
Space Debris Mitigation Guidelines of the
Committee on the Peaceful Uses of Outer
Space
Title 14 of the Code of Federal Regulations (14
CFR), part 460
Treaty on Principles Governing the Activities
of States in the Exploration and Use of
Outer Space, including the Moon and Other
Celestial Bodies (also known as the Outer
Space Treaty)

Websites
Astriagraph: *http://astria.tacc.utexas.edu/
AstriaGraph/*
Beyond Earth Institute*: https://beyondearth.org/*

*Code of Conduct for the International Space
Station Crew: https://www.law.cornell.edu/cfr/
text/14/1214.403*
European Space Agency: *https://www.esa.int/*
*Indian Space Research Organisation (ISRO),
Department of Space: https://www.isro.gov.in/*
Japan Aerospace Exploration Agency (JAXA):
https://global.jaxa.jp/
National Aeronautics and Space Administration
(NASA): *https://www.nasa.gov/*
NASA Space Place for Kids: *https://www.nasa.
gov/learning-resources/for-students-grades-
5-8/* and *https://www.nasa.gov/learning-
resources/for-students-grades-9-12*
Space.com: *https://www.space.com/*
SpaceWatch.Global: *https://spacewatch.global*
United Nations Office for Outer Space Affairs:
https://www.unoosa.org/oosa/index.html

INDEX

Italic page numbers refer to illustrations.